Why, Father?

Also by Toni Maguire

Don't Tell Mummy
When Daddy Comes Home
Helpless
Nobody Came
Don't You Love Your Daddy?
Can't Anyone Help Me?
Pretty Maids All In A Row
They Stole My Innocence
Did You Ever Love Me?
Daddy's Little Girl
Silent Child
Please Protect Us
No Going Home
Won't You Love Me?

Why, Father?

Betrayed by those meant to love me, this is
my true story of survival

TONI
MAGUIRE

with Gerri Mayo

First published in the UK by John Blake Publishing
an imprint of Bonnier Books UK
4th Floor, Victoria House
Bloomsbury Square
London WC1B 4DA
England

Owned by Bonnier Books
Sveavägen 56, Stockholm, Sweden

www.facebook.com/johnblakebooks
twitter.com/jblakebooks

First published in 2023 by John Blake Publishing

Paperback ISBN: 978-1-78946-590-7
Ebook ISBN: 978-1-78946-591-4
Audiobook ISBN: 978-1-78946-592-1

British Library Cataloguing-in-Publication Data:
A CIP catalogue record for this book is available from the British Library.

Design by www.envydesign.co.uk

Printed and bound in Great Britain by Clays Ltd, Elcograf S.p.A

1 3 5 7 9 10 8 6 4 2

Text copyright © Toni Maguire and Gerri Mayo

John Blake Publishing is an imprint of Bonnier Books UK
www.bonnierbooks.co.uk

I would like to thank Toni Maguire for taking me under her wing and believing in me.

This is for my mam, who went to join the angels far too soon, and for my dearest, dearest brother Peter, who has gone to keep her company. Both loved and missed every day.

This is also for Holly, who rescued me from the evil, evil foster parents.

But most of all, I want to thank my wonderful husband, Paul, who has cared, loved and put the broken pieces back together again. I am so lucky and happy now.

A Mother's Warning

Siren wailing, blue lights flashing
A hand grips mine
Tightly holding
Gently warming
Don't let go!
Hospital theatre
Drifting, dreaming
Cradle of arms
Soft singing in my ear
Whispers of warning
'Don't blame your perpetrators
Blame will rebound
Daughter of sin, teller of falsehoods
Crawl into your world of shame
You are the one to blame.'
Don't go to that place
Where guilt and fear abound
Where your world will turn around
Soft singing, warm caress
I awake and find you gone
Never to return
An empty space, a lonely hand
A lost embrace

By Amanda Laurence

Prologue

Knowing that her small sons were being looked after by a neighbour, the woman moved as quietly as she could from the front door to the closed one leading into the parlour. Her body shook as she heard the sounds coming from inside. She had suspected for some time what happened when she was out working. It was not long after the visitor arrived in the village, the one who had brought evil into their home.

She leant against the wall, feeling much of her strength leaving her body. It was not just the horror of what was going on behind that door that shook her so badly, but also the guilt refusing to still its accusing voice. A voice that was asking her why she had done nothing to put a stop to what was happening in her own home A voice now shrieking at her insistently that the time had come to take action.

You know, don't you? the voice of her conscience told her angrily enough to make her gasp for breath as it repeated again that terrible sins were taking place under her roof.

You can't deny it any longer. Unplug your ears and listen to what is taking place here. A command that, reluctantly, she obeyed. Her denial of the sins being committed behind that door had come to an end. She knew when she heard the grunts and gasps of not just one man but two that she had to act. Their sounds and those of a child's whimpers told her just one thing: that the evil was now being shared between two men.

Evil that they were forcing onto her young daughter.

But she was too frightened to open the door and scream at those inside the small room that she wanted them to stop whatever they were doing. She would be cursed by the man whose black robes gave him power over the people in the village.

For didn't he preach the words of God to his congregation even that Sunday?

Didn't he baptise their children?

And didn't he stand beside the grave where a loved one was being buried, asking God for his blessing?

No, she told herself, there was not one person who would believe her. They would just point their finger at her and say she was mad. Or even worse, that it was her, not them, who was committing an unforgivable sin. That heinous one; uttering blasphemous words about a Man of God.

There was only one way out, but first she must make sure her children would leave this place forever. She had already decided she would not be going with them but before she left, she must make sure that all four would be looked after and protected with kindness for the rest of their childhoods. She could only pray that her plan would work. The solution she had come to had to take place that very night, but first, when her daughter was released from the room, she would calm her, wash her body gently and make her clean again. And then, knowing she had made her family safe, she would leave this place forever.

Earlier that evening, Mary finally finished work and wearily began to make her way home. Mrs McFay, the bedridden and frail old woman she cared for every day, was now safely tucked up in her bed. Her daughter had arrived to spend the weekend with her mother, which made Mary thankful that she now had two days free from those responsibilities. Having said her goodbyes, she began walking back home.

Dawn had only just broken that morning when she crawled out of bed to cook breakfast for her family. Then she got all four of her children dressed and made sandwiches for her husband to take to work. It was now twelve hours since she had left the house, after leaving her two youngest with her neighbour Maureen, while the two older ones made their way to school.

That day, the last tinge of heat coming from a faint sun had already disappeared, leaving in its place a damp mist that fell over her head and shoulders. She felt it was that which added to the pain she experienced when she placed one foot in front of the other; it was as though every single bone in her body was aching. The day had not been an easy one, for the old lady had wanted everything just so as her daughter was coming. Bedding must be changed and after a thorough wash, she insisted on her best clean nightdress. All this involved lifting her so many times and Mary's back had taken too much strain. Even her neck hurt when she tried to turn it and all she wanted was to get back and put her feet up with a cup of tea in front of the range in the kitchen, if only for a few minutes. And then she would collect her youngest children from Maureen and slip her a little money that paid for their food.

Not that Maureen would have asked for it. She knew she was more than fortunate in marrying Dennis, the tall red-haired man she had known since they met at Sunday School, one of those men who made no bones about adoring his wife and children. Not only that, he was also one of those rare men who on a Friday evening walked past the pubs where his workmates went so that he could hand over his unopened pay packet to his wife. She was the one in the household who did the budgeting and he was glad of that.

Whereas Mary's husband, Patrick, was a very different sort of man. The lights in the village pub beckoned him in from the moment his fingers curled around his small brown pay packet. Not that he was the only man in the village who believed that having a drink or two after work was more important than making sure their wains were fed. Mary knew that Maureen thought she worked too hard and did her best to help her and her family as much as she could. Which was what the women in the villages did. They, as their mothers had done before them, looked out for each other.

Of course Mary knew that Maureen blamed Patrick's drinking for Mary having to work such long hours to feed the family, even though she had told her more than once that she enjoyed her work. She felt it benefited both the ones who needed care as well as her liking the independence of having earned her own money. She was also genuinely fond of the old lady who she had known since she was a schoolgirl and her patient had been a popular teacher at the school. One who beneath her strict demeanour was kindly even though she made it clear she would not stand for any nonsense in her classroom. Mary was fourteen when she had picked some flowers and dropped in to see Mrs McFay, as the pupils called her, just after she retired – 'Best call me Cathleen now as I'm not your teacher anymore,' she said with a broad smile when she saw the flowers. Having been told that she was welcome to visit whenever she liked, Mary soon found herself enjoying the older woman's company, and she began to visit more frequently. It was Cathleen who encouraged Mary to consider nursing as a career once she left school. As the years passed, however, Cathleen became less sprightly. It was when winter came, bringing in treacherous ice along with frost and drifting snow, that Mary would offer to do her shopping or get anything else that was needed. Cathleen agreed, but only during the severest weeks. In the autumn she was always out in her garden, raking up dead leaves and tending her flower beds at the first signs of spring; giving in to old age was not something she considered.

At least that was until a stroke took away her freedom, leaving her dependent on those she once cared for. But Mary still enjoyed her company and even though her face could show little expression because of the partial paralysis, Cathleen still managed to chuckle at some of the stories Mary told her about the goings-on in the village. Right up to the day when she could no longer leave her bed, Cathleen had insisted on attending Mass. It was then, knowing how important the Mass was to her, that the elderly priest came to visit her every Sunday afternoon so that they could pray together and he could administer the sacrament. That was what living in a small Irish community was like back then. People like Cathleen were not put into old people's homes, for their neighbours and friends did their best to keep the elderly near them and part of the close-knit community.

As she drew nearer her house Mary felt a rush of pleasure at the thought of spending time with her children that weekend as well as attending church on Sunday. Like Cathleen, attending the services had always been important to her, though both she and her patient found it disappointing that the old priest, Father Joseph, who both women had known for a very long time, had now left. He had told his congregation that finally he had given in to the fact that he was now too frail to stand for more than a few minutes at the pulpit. He was going to join other priests like him in a retirement home attached to the monastery where he had trained. The week before he left, he had introduced his replacement. Father Pat was much younger and certainly appeared to be energetic. Mary had already seen him riding his bicycle around the area, stopping to talk to as many people as he could.

She, with her family, had attended his first service. Seated on one of the hard wooden pews, she had listened intently to the young priest's melodious voice. His voice was powerful enough to carry every syllable into all corners of the ancient stone church, yet unlike the other priests Mary had met, there was something about him that she could not put a finger on that stopped her feeling any warmth towards him. When his deep mahogany eyes met hers and his lips lifted into a friendly smile, of course she smiled back. She knew she should take a liking to him and encouraged herself to make more of an effort.

Maybe, she told herself, *it's only because you were so fond of the one who had baptised you and told the children Bible stories when they went to Sunday School.*

Yes, maybe it was just that.

I was born in the mid-1960s, the eldest of four children. Then came Michael, Peter and Keith – all boys apart from me. It seemed that Mum popped one out every twelve months. Which was really pretty usual in the remote Catholic part of Northern Ireland where we lived. I'm sure the neighbours assumed we were quite a normal family, whatever 'normal' was.

We lived in an old stone building which had once, a couple of decades earlier, housed chickens. Which in the county side of Ireland is not as unusual as it might sound. Once a farmer inherited the house from his father, he nearly always seemed to want to have a modern one built in its place. Then it was goodbye to the old croft with its thick stone walls and small windows, where on chilly days and dark evenings condensation trickled down the panes.

The only room with any heat was where one of those old black stoves sat in a wall cavity. Fuelled by peat rather than coal, all the cooking was done on them. When its doors were opened and the peat was poked about a bit, the heat would finally warm the room. After living there, I can't say I blame the young farmers for wanting to build a more modern house. Central heating had arrived and they were eager to have homes where every room was warm all year-round. No longer would they be shivering with the cold when they had to visit the outside lavatory.

My father was lucky getting our home. The farmer's younger brother, wanting a bigger place of his own, had taken over the old croft, partitioned off the cavernous space to make a parlour and bedrooms upstairs, cleaned it up and put in decent floors. Then, not long after he moved in, he had met a woman from Dublin who had no intention of living in the countryside. This happened just when my parents were getting married and rather than let the house stand empty, they were able to live there for a reasonable rent.

Ma made it as comfy as she could. She found some secondhand furniture, sewed cushions for the chairs, colourful quilts for the beds and had vases full of fresh flowers, which she dried to add colour throughout the year. In winter our pyjamas hung on a clothes rack in front of the stove so they were warm when we slipped them on, as were our beds, which she heated by filling stone water bottles. When we woke we'd find ice on our bedroom windows and see the plumes of our smoke-like breath floating in front of us. It was so cold, there was nothing we could do but pull on as many of our clothes as we could, under our bedding.

The way we lived was normal in that sprawling village, which also included the cluster of farm cottages. My ma had once worked as a nurse. A career that came partly to an end when I was just a tiny bulge. But having the spirit of one who is called to care for others, she quickly found a different type of nursing: looking after the elderly whose families had crossed the water to work in England. That might have been a country that the elderly had little time for, but they could hardly complain about the money that was sent to them. It was those extra pounds that paid for their heating and care when they needed it.

Life for the children in our village was much the same for all of us. Well before we started school we were playing outside in the road, where the eyes of the community watched out for us. Did those children believe that danger might suddenly be brought in by a stranger? I don't know if they did, but I do know that they never gave a thought that it might come from someone much closer.

Someone who would steal all the joy of childhood from a trusting small person.

I must have been around five or maybe even younger when I was looked at by my father with something called desire. Not that a child who has only just begun school would recognise that particular expression on an adult's face any more than they would have any idea over the next few months that they were being groomed. That was hardly a word they would know, let alone understand what it meant. I know I wouldn't have, but I certainly do now.

As I came to learn, the most important part of grooming is earning a child's trust. Though if that child is one of their children, that's hardly a problem to begin with. They know what makes a small girl beam with pleasure: it's when she hears compliments from someone she looks up to. Such as being told she is looking so pretty when she's wearing her Sunday dress. Then there's another one which is only spoken to her in private; imagine a large adult male's hand stroking her gently on the cheek and a deep voice telling her she's his special little girl. That makes her feel so proud, right up to the time when she finds out what being special means to the man who is saying it.

Of course, as a small child I had no understanding that the affection Da was giving me was all part of his plan. It begins with an arm around the shoulder, a gentle hug and little games such as being tickled on the stomach and under the arms, which ends in gales of laughter and a hand roaming freely over the little body.

And it doesn't take long for a kiss to come. One not on the cheek or the top of the head, but on her lips: 'For my special girl,' he tells her, 'and let's keep that a secret between you and me.' She might look rather puzzled by that command, because she knows it is one, but still she nods her head in agreement. Then he is reassured that the first step of his grooming has succeeded.

Soon, he feels complacently, their secret will be a much bigger one. One he is impatient to commence. Not that the child will be as happy as he will be. But that's not a thought that he allows to enter his head. Not for one moment does he consider the harm he might do to her. Harm that can last a lifetime.

No doubt when she is a little older and he becomes more persistent, she will sense that what he is doing is wrong. Then she will use up the remains of her courage telling him she's not happy and that she wants him to stop. A small act of defiance but he has already worked out how, over the years of her being under his roof, he will overcome it. The words 'emotional blackmail' might not be in his vocabulary but he cunningly knows what small remarks he can make over time that will frighten her a little. Yes, he needs to make her see the harm she would do to herself, should she talk. He will use phrases such as 'who will believe you?' or tell her that people wouldn't want to hear stories like that, or maybe nice girls don't talk about private parts of their body, never, ever. And if she did say something, the other parents would stop their children mixing with her, and even worse for her future, if the parents complained to the school that she was a bad influence, the head might well decide to expel her. And as for getting a job without qualifications ... well, that was unlikely. She would carry the blame for what she had said for years.

That is why it has to remain their secret. Though so far, with her being so young, all she can learn is that their secret must be kept.

When the next kiss is even more forceful than all the ones given to her before and his hand slides down beneath her waistband, he repeats that she mustn't share their secret with anyone else. As those words leave his lips he can tell by the expression in her eyes that his seemingly gentle command has become cemented in the little girl's brain. That makes him feel safe. Now he can begin to press ahead with those desires that have troubled him for so long. For each day he becomes more confident that soon he will have enough control over her to make her obey him.

So how do I know how the minds of men like that work? Because it happened to me. I was one of the far too many children who believe everything adults tell them.

Now my memory of how it all started is understandably a little vague but considering everything that happened in our family occurred before I turned eight, that is hardly surprising. I seem to remember one of Da's excuses for me to keep quiet was that he didn't want us to make my younger brothers jealous.

'Can't have them thinking my wee girl's the favourite with their da, now can we?' he would say with a wink, which made me giggle as any little girl would.

Considering two of my brothers were little more than babies that hardly made much sense but then I was too pleased to be getting so much attention to give it a thought. After all, he was my father, so that meant he loved me, didn't it? And anything he told me had to be true. A belief that had disappeared well before I turned eight.

Now I don't want it to sound as though every day of my childhood was a bad one because I do have some happy memories which are immensely important to me. One that often springs to mind is waking up to hear Ma singing 'Happy Birthday' to me as she drew my bedroom curtains. It was when I turned six. As my birthday wasn't on a weekend I had to go to school with Michael, who at 5 years old had just started there himself, only this time Ma had taken the day off, which meant that for once, she was free to walk there with us.

As I was having my hair brushed and put into a neat ponytail, she had told me that there would be presents waiting for me when I returned home. And our neighbour Maureen's family would be coming over for tea as well, so it would be a real celebration.

'So we will be having a little party for you, darlin',' she said as she gave me a big hug and told me to come straight home later on because there would also be a surprise waiting for me.

'What is it?'

'If I tell you, it won't be a surprise, now will it?'

'No, Ma.'

'Well then, you'll just have to wait a little,' she said, laughing at me as she gave my ponytail a little tug and set it swinging. 'Off you go now.'

And grinning away, Michael and I walked into the playground to join our friends.

It wasn't long after entering the classroom with all my chattering classmates that I found out they all knew it was my birthday. No sooner had I sat down at the small wooden desk than one of the girls came over and with a beaming smile handed me a huge card, which the whole class had managed to sign.

If that wasn't a great start to my day, it got even better when my teacher and the whole class sang 'Happy Birthday, Gerri' to me. I must say that was one of my best days at school. Not that I can remember much about the lessons we had, just that once we had our lunch, I was impatient to go home. Nothing to do with not wanting to be at school, more the thought of those presents waiting for me and finding out what the big surprise was.

'Do you know what Ma meant when she said there was a surprise for me?' I asked Michael.

He just shrugged.

'You do, don't you?'

No answer, just another exaggerated shrug of his shoulders, which made me convinced my brother was in on the plot.

'Well, let's get back,' I said impatiently as I walked as fast as I could back home, with Michael grinning away alongside me.

Our parents were both sitting down in the kitchen when we went in but there was no sign of any surprise as my eyes swept the room, looking for it. Then my father, appearing as nonchalant as he could, went out of the room and in just a few seconds he returned, holding the cutest little grey kitten I had ever seen.

I gasped with pleasure when he gently placed her in my arms.

'Happy Birthday,' he said and I simply beamed up at him. This was the nicest present I could have thought of. I was in love with her from the very first moment my fingers felt the softness of her fur. I couldn't believe she was mine.

'Now give your old da a kiss,' he instructed and of course I gave him one when he placed his cheek near my mouth.

My brothers came over to where I was sitting, wanting to stroke her too.

'Be gentle with her,' Ma warned as she saw their little hands descend on the kitten's fur, 'she's only a wee baby.'

Ma looked so pretty that day. Her light brown hair was curling round her face and those blue eyes of hers were sparkling as she smiled away when she saw how delighted I was with my furry present. I think now that part of the reason my mother was so happy was because Da appeared like a truly caring father.

She had really gone to town for that birthday. Not only had she baked a big cake and written 'Happy Birthday' on it in pink icing, she must have spent hours making me a beautiful light blue dress. It had a full skirt, cap sleeves and a gorgeous white collar. I insisted on running upstairs to get out of my school uniform and try it on. Once she slipped it over my head, I just about skipped around the room with delight.

My next present was another one from Ma: a blonde-haired doll with, as she said with a smile, 'blue eyes just like mine.' Ma must have made her dress too for she was wearing one that was a smaller but identical version of the pale blue one I had just put on.

A little later, when plates of food had been put out on the table, Maureen and her children – Robert and Dennis (named after his father), who were about the same age as Michael and me – arrived, bearing presents. They were all the usual things that little girls are given: a colouring book, a packet of crayons and sweets, which my brothers looked at hopefully.

That was the beginning of a new year for me and when a picture of that day flashes through my mind, it makes me smile a little. It's one I try to keep hold of because it was just before other ones that still give me nightmares crept into my short life.

That was also the year our much-loved priest left and the new younger one came into our village.

A man who changed all of our lives.

And not for the better.

For a few weeks after my birthday I was a very happy little girl. I had my purring playful kitten that I named Flo. There were a few friends who lived nearby that I could play with at weekends and for a while both my parents seemed to be in good spirits.

Da's car might have been what we would now call 'a bit of an old banger', but at Easter, which was late that spring, he drove us all to the beach at Murlough Bay. A beautiful five-mile stretch of golden shoreline near the stunning Mourne Mountains, which were covered in deep gorse and grass. Sheep munched away contentedly on those slopes and I could see tiny spots of yellow, which my mother told me were the flowers that grew on gorse at that time of the year.

It was one of those days which I can still picture now. My two older brothers and me running along the golden sand, while Keith, the youngest, was carried by Ma. The wind was blowing our hair all over the place as we ran on the long stretch of sand while our parents looked for a sheltered place for us to picnic. Ma had packed food and soft drinks. There were thick sandwiches filled with chicken, and some cheese and chutney in others, as well as a flask of tea and bottles of lemonade for us children. There was also a blanket, which was laid out when she decided that they had found a good spot.

'Have to be careful with this wind not to be eating sand sandwiches,' she told us laughingly.

With a bit of help from Ma we all took off our shoes and ran back down to the edge of the sea. After we had gone paddling, we watched with some amazement as a group of teenage boys ran on the sands, multicoloured kites flying high in the clear blue sky. Next, we decided to try and build a sandcastle although as each layer was built, the wind took it away, making us shriek with laughter. Afterwards, despite the wind, we all managed to tuck into our picnic before it was time to go home.

That's another nice memory. There is only one other that I really treasure and it occurred a little later.

It was a few months after my birthday when both Cathleen's and my life began to change. My mother tried to explain to me the effect of Cathleen's stroke that had resulted in her ending up in hospital – she wanted me to understand why, when Cathleen came home, Ma would have to work much longer hours for a while.

'So you won't be here when I come back from school?' I asked, disappointed.

With my brothers going over to Maureen's to play when we returned from school, sometimes it was just Ma and me in the house, which made me so happy because I loved having her all to myself. Being with her without any interruptions from my three younger brothers was so rare but I cherished those times.

Left alone, I would chatter away to Ma. Not that I can remember what it was about now. I know she would ask about my day and look at any drawings I had done at school before pinning them up on the wall. While she made supper, she would sing to me, my favourite song being 'Funny Face', which made us both giggle. I can remember other songs she sang as well ('Danny Boy' was a favourite); she had such a pretty and melodic voice. Even now I can hear those songs in my head and I summon them up when I feel blue.

Little wonder she heard the note of sadness in my voice when she tried to explain why Cathleen needed her more. Over and over I asked why she was not going to be home so much. Seeing the look on my face, she gave me a huge hug and kissed the top of my head.

'Now, darlin', you must be a big girl and understand that I need to spend more time there when Cathleen comes out of hospital. She's really poorly. But it won't be for long, just till she's a little better. Now don't worry that you'll be all alone in the house. I've already arranged for you and Michael to go to Maureen's if your da's not back from work by then. And you like it over there, don't you?'

'Yes,' I answered hesitantly. Truth to tell, although I liked everyone over there, I found that with Maureen's sons and my three brothers, it was far too noisy and boisterous. Not that Maureen seemed in the least bit bothered – she was one of those women who loved having children around her.

'Good, that's settled then and either me or your father will come over and collect all of you later in the day.'

What Ma didn't tell me was that she would be working quite a few weekends too. Rita, Cathleen's only daughter, who had children of her own as well as a husband and a full-time job in a recruitment agency, could only manage travelling down from Belfast Airport after she caught the flight from Glasgow once a month. She had managed to take time off work as soon as she heard her mother was in hospital.

Had I been old enough to understand just what the results can be for an elderly woman having a stroke, I might have been more aware that Ma was not going to be home early for some time to come. A little later, I learnt that Cathleen's recovery was not progressing very well and in fact it looked like she would need 24-hour care for some time. Rita and Ma had turned Cathleen's dining room into a bedroom as going up and down stairs was now impossible. – 'But then she's a courageous woman who's not going to give up without a fight,' I heard her tell Rita on the phone.

* * *

When Ma told me my da was also happy with the arrangement, I truly believed Da was just being kind until I worked out why he was happy for Ma to be out of the house when I came back from school. I know he told her that the boys would be fine at Maureen's and as she was earning more, they could afford to give our neighbour a little more money to feed all three of them. And if he was working, then I could go over there too. Though knowing how I liked spending time with my kitten, he would get my tea if he was back in time.

'It's just terrible for her, she was so active,' I heard

Ma saying to Da, who muttered something about it being a real shame.

'Seeing as you'll be working longer hours in the evening, I'll come and collect you. And if it's a very late night, I'll put the children to bed first. I can always ask Maureen to slip over for a few minutes while I go and get you. Otherwise we can pick them up on the way back so don't worry about that,' he added.

I can understand why she thought he was being kind; I did as well, but after a few months I knew it pleased him to know exactly what time Ma would be home for he had his own plans. Apart from visiting Cathleen at the hospital and meeting up with Rita, who had been adamant about paying Ma for all the hours spent with her mother, they needed to sort out the arrangements for what would happen next after Cathleen came home. The dining-room furniture needed to be moved out and stored; the Red Cross supplied a hospital bed and commode.

* * *

Over those free days of hers, Ma walked Michael and me to school, which pleased me no end as I simply loved spending time with her. I envied Maureen's children having their mother home all day and just wished Ma could be like that as well. Especially when I could see that when she had more energy, she had time to read to me once I was tucked up in bed. But the days went by too fast and suddenly she disappeared from the house from early morning until quite late at night. For at least two days a week, and often more, it was just my father and me in the house.

As soon as we got home from school Michael would ask if he could go over to Maureen's. Not that he needed to ask, for I soon came to realise that was exactly what Da wanted him to do: 'Off you go, lad,' he would say each time, 'and I'll pick you and your brothers up before I go and fetch your mother. Have to get you all into bed first.'

Once he was given permission, Michael would sprint out of the house.

'Look both ways before you cross the road, mind,' Da would shout.

It was on those afternoons that Da became very affectionate and he would stroke my back and hug me. To begin with, I liked him being like that – it made me feel loved. Though I didn't like those 'grown-up kisses', as he called them. They were all wet and sloppy, I just wanted to wipe my mouth afterwards. But still, to me they might have felt a bit disgusting, but up until then my father had done nothing to scare me and that was something he was quite careful not to do. He understood that each move had to be introduced slowly so that there were no hysterical objections for Ma to see or hear about.

That is what grooming is all about.

Soon those gentle caresses were not enough and slowly over the weeks they began to become a little more forceful. It was then that I started to feel nervous when I finished school and I'd try to avoid being near Da or left alone with him. I would say I'd been invited over to a friend's house – though only a few seemed to meet with his approval – or offer up whatever excuse I could find. How I wished Ma would stop working those long hours but nothing seemed to have changed at Cathleen's house and Da seemed quite content with Ma's long daily absences. It certainly brought a little extra money into the house, which I'm sure pleased him.

I used to keep my fingers crossed that Da would still be at work when I returned home from school. When there wasn't any sign of him I just about gulped with relief before following Michael as quickly as I could over the road to where my two little brothers were. Even if he returned fairly soon after, he could hardly come over and remove me without taking all of us, so I felt safe there.

But there were at least two days a week when, as I neared the house and saw his old car parked outside, my heart would sink. I knew Michael would be told he was free to go and off he would trot, leaving me alone with a smirking father. Oh, the first half-hour or so was perfectly normal. Flo would appear and give me a welcoming greeting by rubbing herself against my ankles and purring loudly. I would cuddle and stroke her until she ran off to play with something she had spotted – she had toys but a leaf or a piece of paper seemed to attract her more. Then Da would ask if I was hungry and make me a sandwich. Nearly every time he would sit on a chair near mine, mug of tea in his hand, making pleasant small talk such as asking me about school and what I had done that day.

It was those conversations that aroused conflicting

emotions in me. I still loved my Da then, just not the things that he did when we were alone together after taking me into the parlour once I had finished eating. Our family life normally revolved around the large kitchen with its big table and of course the range, but the parlour was rarely used and he seemed to think that was the right place to be when he started touching me. It was also a room with a lockable door so if Michael or Ma arrived back unexpectedly, he had time to straighten up. I just hated every time those big hands of his grabbed hold of me and I wanted to squirm away. By then, he almost always smelt of whiskey, a smell that made me recoil as those sloppy kisses landed on my mouth. Still somewhere between the ages of six and seven, I was beginning to feel confused: something was not quite right about what he was doing. But he was my da and wasn't I meant to believe what he told me, which was that fathers did these things with special little girls?

When memories of those times flash into my mind, I can almost smell his breath and hear his voice: 'Come here, darlin', don't you want to please your da then?' I can see my younger self standing there, hands twisting the fabric of my school skirts nervously, still not knowing what to say. And in the end I said yes – what else could I have said then?

'So come over here then,' he would say, giving me his friendly da smile and sweeping me up and perching me on his knee. I would snuggle up a little then for I always hoped that was as much as he was going to do, because some days it was only that.

Looking back, I can see what he was aiming for.

I still have a very good memory of every step he made to do what he wished to me, while making sure he kept his control over me. Memories that I have never been able to banish from my mind. They are with me in my waking hours and I cry if one pops up unexpectedly. I might be watching TV or listening to the radio and suddenly I'm back in that parlour. These images resurface often in my dreams and my nightmares – I can wake to find the mattress has shifted because of their violence.

And what did happen? To begin with it was a hand running up my leg past my knee until he went further up and stroked that place between them that I was old enough to think of as private. I wanted to wriggle away but like a little puppet, I let him pull my strings and so I stayed where I was.

Another way of him getting me close to him was to say, 'Look what I've got for you, Gerri,' and I would see his hand sliding into his pocket and coming out, holding half a crown. 'That's for you to buy sweeties with, because you're such a good little girl,' he would say. 'Now come over here and thank me.' Then the coin would be pressed into my hand before his mouth came back onto mine as his hand slid high up under my school skirt.

I wanted to tell him to stop then, but what child has the courage to stand up for themselves in those circumstances? I know I didn't. Though I wish I had, because it didn't take long for him to want more. It was around then, when I was losing my confidence and he was gaining more, that he went further. I had not even turned seven when he first began to take hold of my hands and force my little fingers around that ugly part of his body that I did not want to touch. My ears felt assaulted as he whispered instructions of what he wanted those fingers of mine to do.

'This is another secret between us,' he told me, giving me a hug once it was over. 'Only special girls get to do this.'

I began to wish I wasn't in the least bit special. Especially when he told me the reason why I must keep another secret: 'Now listen to me,' he said. 'If you and other special little girls tell others their secrets, they won't be spoken to again. Now you wouldn't want that to happen, would you?'

No, I wouldn't, not at all; I almost burst into tears at the very thought. Though in fact, back when I was a child, there was a lot of truth in what he told me. So when I looked at other girls in my school and wondered which ones were the special girls, I never asked them because I would have been devastated if they had shut me out and refused to talk to me. The secret was beginning to take away the last of my childhood happiness. How I hated the smell of that sticky stuff that coated my hands when I was sent from the parlour to wash them in the kitchen sink. And my ears stung from those horrid gasping sounds he made when I did as he asked. They were the same ones I had heard seeping through the walls of the bedroom where he and Ma slept.

When I was curled up in bed as tightly as I could, my dreams now always seemed to turn into nightmares that woke my mother in the middle of the night. The question

I've often asked myself is whether Ma had any suspicion about what was happening. Maybe, but hopefully not as early as that. But didn't she see that I was changing? No longer that laughing little child who chattered nonstop, instead my dreams tortured me.

When she heard me cry out in the night and came into my room, she must have noticed from the bedding that had fallen to the floor that my sleep had been badly disturbed. But she never asked if anything was troubling me. Instead she tucked me back in, kissed the top of my head and murmured that I should sleep well.

7

Da must have believed that he was getting away with his crime. For a crime it was.

Now my father, being a Catholic who had been brought up by a family who never missed church, surely must have been aware that he was also going against the rules that were laid out in the Old Testament. Beneath his composure, I think this was troubling him, but not enough to stop him.

He had waited some time to decide I was ready for him to take the final step: intercourse. Not that he called it that, he just told me that it was something that made fathers and daughters closer. One day he knocked back some whiskey, which was unlikely to have been his first drink, and then, telling me to open my mouth, he tipped his glass so that the remainder of the liquid slipped down, burning my throat.

I might not have liked the taste to begin with, but it spread warmth through my body and made me drowsy. Though not drowsy enough not to feel the sharp pain in my lower body when he finally did as he wanted.

I was not to know that what my da was doing was a very big sin.

And what do good Catholics do if they don't want to be punished by God?

They go to confession.

They sit down in small wooden cupboard-like place in the church; the one where the priest sits behind a screen made of opaque material, which is designed to make both sides anonymous.

That was the idea then, though in our somewhat remote village, where there was just one priest, it was only the confessor who might not be recognised. Whereas the priest who had baptised all of us would have known by the voice exactly who was sitting on the other side of the partition, his successor would not have done so. My father must have been the only person in the village who was pleased to see the old priest go and a new and younger one take his place; Da's voice was unknown to him, which must have made my father feel free to confess what he was doing to me.

8

The people in the village were full of talk about the new priest. They said how he had called on so many families already to introduce himself. It was the elderly, who had been so fond of the old priest and less open to change, who were, within a couple of weeks of him taking over the role, beginning to speak highly of him. Friends and neighbours were told how kind and thoughtful he had been when they invited him in for the obligatory cup of tea and a slice of homemade cake – 'The Young Father Patrick' as they now called him, had already expressed some new ideas which showed just how dedicated he was in wanting to do good things for the village.

He had certainly been smart enough to make sure he won over all those who had known the old priest for so many years. There were quite a few tears when they attended his last sermon and said their goodbyes. And people often put up a barrier against a much-liked person's replacement. A barrier that in this case hardly seemed to last more than a week or so. This priest, with his boyish good looks and a shy but engaging charm, somehow managed to ingratiate himself as he had conversations with those almost old enough to be his grandparents. However much the former priest was missed, when the locals heard the older villagers they respected speak so highly of the new one, they took notice and repeated this praise to others. Within a matter of a few days he had managed to earn the glowing reputation of being a good Christian man dedicated to his new flock. One who they believed would be an asset to the village.

Another progressive idea that the new priest was putting forward to younger families with small children was to start a Sunday School. Although the Methodists and the Anglicans had them, in the Catholic Church this was very rare, and he was asking people what they thought – 'Now don't you think that would be a fine idea for the wee ones? Sure, then they could be learning all those grand Bible stories.'

There was a mixture of responses to that particular suggestion. Some did not want to copy the Protestants, while others thought it would be a good way of keeping their children occupied on a Sunday. Not that the priest was concerned about their opinion, for this was clearly one of his cunning ways of finding out which families had small daughters. He must have felt quite secure that in using that approach, not one person would have a clue about the real reason he wanted to find out about the children in his parish. People just appreciated the fact that he made the effort to call on them and not only shared his ideas, but seemed to listen intently to their opinions.

I guess after each visit this man was able to make a

mental note of all the families who had a daughter well under the age of ten. Those were the ones he would have made sure to visit often. Though not just them at first; he was wise enough to know this might be noticed. He must have known that a little patience would eventually prove worthwhile because when he found that man whose voice he recognised, he would discover someone with the same lascivious desires as himself. Someone he must have wanted to find for a long time. Just listening to my father's first confession must have given him such a thrill. It makes me feel sick and even now I flush with humiliation at the very thought of it.

Not that I had any idea of what was said in the confessional, but now I can guess. The first time, I imagine my father would have spoken of his thoughts when he saw his daughter. I'm pretty certain he uttered those thoughts cautiously. Before he gave any details of those desires of his, he would have needed to know if it was safe to continue. I doubt if he was too concerned for although there had been talks in Ireland (and it would be decided by Rome) about relaxing the Catholic Church's rules about what would happen when heinous sins were confessed, so far there had hardly been any agreement on that idea: Instead, priests who diligently listened to their parishioners' confessions – mostly about consuming alcohol, the odd fight and sometimes giving their wife a beating (unbelievably this was OK in the eyes of the law right up until well past the seventies) – insisted the giving of the right advice and offering absolution was their duty whereas making a phone call to the Garda was not in any way covered by the vows they had taken. Their point was that if people didn't feel safe in the confessional, then they would simply cease to enter it or else sanitise their confession.

'It would take away their trust in us, and missing confession could be bad for their souls,' was something I heard more than one person saying.

A lucky decision for my father, but a very unlucky one for me.

Since then there have been documentaries on TV, newspaper articles and books written about those involved in abuse and just what happens to a priest who himself has broken not just the law, but the rules of the Church too. Everything I've seen on TV or read about has shown me that the Church applies their punishments with little, if any, outside help. I, like many other people, believe far too much was covered up back then, for maybe one reason: they did not want people to lose their trust in the Church.

My father certainly must have quickly found that he was safe confessing the thoughts in his head which disturbed him only a little, for he couldn't have found a better person to listen to him with a show of compassion that was clearly false. Not that he'd have had any knowledge of that to begin with, though that didn't stop Da from continuing to put his hands and lips all over me.

Each time the priest visited, he must have known my mother was out. To begin with, I just wondered why he had come again – after all, there were so many other homes to get tea and biscuits from.

It took barely longer than three weeks after he'd started visiting all the families in the village for me to find out.

Of course I hadn't the slightest suspicion the first time my father told me to open the door to the priest. He had seen through the window that we had a visitor and who it was – 'It'll be you he'll want to see,' Da told me. 'Most probably wants to hear what you'll think of him starting a Sunday School, seeing you and Michael are about the right age for it.'

Somehow I sensed a little nervousness in his voice but then that would hardly have been surprising. He was not to know that our new priest was hell-bent on finding the man who had confessed his sin of having dreams about committing incest. Not a thought that would have entered many people's heads, was it? So I should think he was on tenterhooks about his voice being recognised.

'Off you go, Gerri, before he has to knock on the door,' he said when he saw me hesitating, 'and you be sure to welcome him in.'

I suppose like most children, I was in awe of those men

in their black robes, who everyone seemed to think were wonderful.

When I pulled the door open, I received a beaming smile as he bent down and told me his name was Father Patrick – 'Or "Father Pat", as most people seem to call me. Now what's your name?' he asked as he took hold of my small hand and gave it a gentle shake.

'Gerri,' I answered, a blush staining my cheeks.

'And what a pretty little thing you are too!' And I received another smile as he continued: 'Nice meeting you, Gerri. Now is your mother in?'

I shook my head and said she was still at work but my father was at home. And just to prove it, Da appeared behind me and invited him in.

More hand shaking as my father told him it was only he and I in the house and that Ma wasn't due back for a while as she was at work.

'Oh, what work does she do?' Father Pat asked once he was inside and being shown into the parlour.

'Well, she used to be a nurse before we started our wee family. Now she cares for people who need to be looked after in their own homes.'

He then mentioned Cathleen's name and how she had a bad stroke and that my mother was there from early in the morning as she had to take over from the night carer.

'So your wife's out till quite late then?'

'I'm afraid so, Father.'

It didn't take the priest long to ask if I had any siblings. My father went on to tell him about how they stayed at

Maureen's house until he or Ma went over the road to fetch them – 'Don't know what we'd do without a good neighbour like her.'

'So you have three little boys and Gerri's the eldest child? I should think your pretty little daughter just might be the apple of your eye,' he said, giving me another of his warm smiles.

'I think so,' my father answered as he gave my shoulder a little squeeze and said how good I was, both in the home and at school.

It was all a completely normal conversation, except it gave the priest nearly all the information he needed. He now knew about the long hours Ma worked, where my brothers were up until bedtime and even which Sundays Ma would be free to go to church. Pretty comprehensive fact gathering for such a brief encounter. After that, he brought up the subject of the morning Sunday School he had in mind: 'There's lots of young children around here, aren't there, Gerri, who might like that, don't you think? Would you like to be going along to that?'

But I only heard the word 'school' and thinking I might end up doing sums or spelling on a Sunday, I doubt if I looked very keen until he told me it was all about listening to stories from the Bible. Now that sounded better, so knowing he wanted me to say yes, I wriggled a bit and nodded: 'I suppose so,' I managed to say.

It was as I answered this question and his remark about 'lots of young children' that I saw a look exchanged between him and Da. Not one I understood, not then.

'Won't be any need for confessions there,' the priest added with a tight little smile and I saw Da's cheeks redden far more than my earlier girlish blushes.

Just as I saw the priest's mouth move to say something more, we all heard Ma's footsteps as she came through the door. Whatever words were about to escape his lips were quickly replaced by him saying, 'I expect I'll see you all at church this Sunday,' as Da went through into the kitchen to greet her.

I heard her explain that she had managed to get back a little early this time because the night carer had arrived sooner than she expected and her husband had kindly driven Ma back.

'Must say, I was grateful to the pair of them. It's been a hard day,' I heard her saying before she entered the parlour. 'Evening, Father,' she said. 'Saw the bicycle outside, so I thought it must be you.'

I'm pretty certain that Ma had to gulp a bit with disappointment when she had seen it. I should think she was dying to put her feet up for a rest, but a priest doesn't come into one's home and leave without being offered both food and drink. I could almost hear her saying goodbye to her small spot of rest, but she managed to give him a warm smile before saying, 'Oh, how kind of you to make a visit. You must be out and about from dawn to dusk, Father. And it doesn't look as though that husband of mine has even made you a cup of tea. Now I'm sure you'd like one?'

'If it's not too much trouble, seeing you've only just got back from work, Mrs O'Brien.'

'No trouble at all, Father. I'm desperate for one myself so it's just as easy to make another – well, three, I suppose,' she said, glancing over at Da with a look of exasperation. 'You two stay in here with Father,' she told us. 'I think I can manage making it on my own.' Not that I had seen my father make any movement to assist her before she turned round, leaving the door open, and walked into the kitchen.

I could hear her scuttling about before she came back with little Flo following at her heels, carrying a tray with a large pot of tea, milk, sugar, a glass of juice for me and a plate of biscuits. This time it was the priest who jumped up, took it from her and carefully placed the tray on the small coffee table. Ma poured out the tea and passed around the biscuits before she sat herself down with a grateful sigh, cup in hand. The conversation about Sunday services and Sunday School was resumed. It was rather boring for me, so I spent the time playing with my kitten.

Boring or not, I can still remember the priest's arrival at our house very clearly. Perched on the edge of his chair, legs pressed tightly together and his little finger raised slightly in the air, he took sips from one of Ma's best china cups.

I think I heard a sigh of relief escape Ma when he eventually stood up and said he had to get on his way, as he had another call to make.

That was the first time he came.

But not the last.

10

When I first met the priest and being too innocent then to possess the ability to see the real person, I know I looked on him with great reverence. Like most other children in our village, I was in awe of what our parents called a Man of God. And did my knees tremble a little when he bent over to shake my hand? Of course they did.

On that day in the confessional when my father wanted to rid himself of his guilty conscience, he must have hoped he would be absolved with a few Hail Marys and the priest's voice telling him, 'You're forgiven,' or whatever was said to those who poured out their guilty secrets. He would have had no idea that he would be talking to a man who would ultimately corrupt him even further. I doubt the priest could believe his luck when my father's guilty words were poured into his ears. There was a man, invisible to him, telling him all about his own darkest desires. Desires that up until then, he believed he was the only man in Ireland to have, for in those days crimes against children were rarely talked about. Mostly, I suspect, because it was usually a relative doing the abusing.

In his own way, I suppose the priest must have been quite an unhappy man. For aren't those who hide their darkness under the guise of the completely different person they pretend to be living a very lonely existence? Not that that excuses his actions in any way, nor can I summon up an ounce of forgiveness for what he did to me. It just explains a certain amount, such as how he managed to fool so many people. For his pretence at being a good Christian fooled a whole small town. Certainly Ma, who had not taken a liking to him initially, came to believe he was a good man. That continued until she too became completely disillusioned. And if he fooled people like her, he certainly hadn't found it difficult to have a little girl, who had only just turned seven, eating out of his hand.

It only took a few smiles and compliments to have me trusting this man and believing not only had he come to our home to introduce himself, but he wanted to get to know me a little. Which he had, but not for the reason he gave me.

11

I was too young to question why, after learning of my mother's working hours, Father Patrick only visited when she was out. But I did wonder why, when Michael and I returned from school one day, he was told to go over to Maureen's, where his two younger brothers were. It was something he usually wanted to do but being old enough to want to meet any visitors, he objected to being told to leave when the priest was due to arrive.

It was after Michael and I had swallowed the last part of our homemade soda bread and jam that Da told him he'd best get over to Maureen's: 'We'll be having a bit of a prayer meeting,' was what he said, though Michael didn't seem to take that in. Instead he jumped up from his chair and, with his chest puffed up and face pink with temper, asked why he had to go when I was allowed to stay.

'If Gerri's allowed to meet him, why can't I too?' he wanted to know. 'She's already met him and I haven't – have I, Da?'

'You will on Sunday,' Da told him, which placed a scowl on Michael's face.

'We will all see him at church, but that's not like seeing him here, is it, Da?'

Father must have suddenly thought how he would make sure that if Michael stayed, he would never want to again: 'Just thought you might be a bit bored,' was his excuse. This earned him a shrug of the shoulders and a half smile.

It was me who saw the priest riding his bike into our yard first.

'I'll go and let him in,' Michael told us as he moved quickly to the door.

It took a few minutes before he and the priest, followed by Flo, who had been warming herself outside in the sun, came into the kitchen. Da said that Michael was excited about meeting him and Father Pat's face creased into that charming smile of his as he asked us the kind of questions that adults do of small children, such as what we had done at school that day. A question I let my brother answer, as I was busy picking Flo up for a cuddle.

'And what's your little pet's name, Gerri?' the priest wanted to know.

I told him and explained that she had been a tiny little kitten when my father had given her to me on my birthday.

'Ah, what a lovely present,' he said.

I noticed that he made no effort to stroke her, which other people nearly always did. Nor, when she was back on the ground, did Flo go anywhere near him.

'Your father's a thoughtful man, knowing how much you would like her.'

To which I answered yes, for I could hardly say that he hardly ever put anyone else before himself, could I? It was Michael's hair he ruffled, not mine this time, as he told him he looked a lot like his father: 'You have your da's dark hair, don't you? And I can see you're going to grow tall and slim just like him.'

'Skinny' might have been the more truthful word, for like Da, even though my brother ate as much as he could, with his sharp elbows and his bony frame Michael remained wiry. Da had hardly an ounce of fat on him then, either. Later he would look much larger, but that was when he was so bloated with all the alcohol he poured down his throat.

That afternoon, Father Pat appeared to be such a harmless man. If anything, I saw him as being rather shy. He was lucky that Flo had managed to give him another topic for him to bring up when he saw me.

Then he changed the subject from asking Michael about school to talking about his ideas for children's Bible studies after Sunday Mass. All of which was boring enough for me, but even more so for a boy who hadn't yet turned six. It was when the two of us were told that it was time for our prayer meeting that my brother looked a little dismayed.

'If you want to, Michael, you can go over to Maureen now,' Da said quietly. 'You've met Father Pat now and that's what you wanted, wasn't it?'

Looking grateful, my brother shot me a pitying smile

and sped off. I just wished I was flying out of the house with him. This was turning out to be a really useless day. Outside the sun was shining and just over the road were my brothers and Maureen's children. Over there I could be playing too and drinking homemade lemonade. But no, I was not offered the choice that Michael had been given. Of course I had not yet come to realise that there was a very good reason for that.

I was the main attraction.

The next stage of that visit was for the three of us to move from the kitchen to the parlour where, before going in, we dipped our fingers in the bowl of holy water by the door. Almost as soon as we entered, Da pulled over two cushions from the settee and told me to kneel on one as he did, because we were about to listen to Father Pat's prayers.

I have to say, I was bored out of my mind. Once they were finished, Da rose up stiffly and I jumped up too, hoping it was all over. But no, the priest had to spout out a short sermon, if that's what I could call it, before his visit was over. I certainly breathed a sigh of relief when he was gone.

I really couldn't see the point in that visit, though I certainly can now.

I hoped this would be the last time he would want to conduct a service in our home.

It wasn't.

12

When Ma arrived home, Da had already left to go and collect the boys – 'I'll get them into bed before she comes,' he told me. 'Give you and your ma a little time together.' Which, as my father being thoughtful was an unusual occurrence, made me feel both surprised and pleased. Having time with Ma on my own was always something I enjoyed. Him getting the boys ready for bed quickly was also a bit of a relief as I didn't want to hear a stream of teasing questions about the priest's prayer meeting coming from Michael. Once Ma arrived and had a cup of tea in her hand, she said that she had heard Father Pat had been over that afternoon.

'So did you enjoy your visit with him, Gerri?' she asked.

'It was all right, I suppose,' I answered sullenly, which made her laugh a little.

'Are you saying him reading parts of the Scripture went on for too long?'

'Yes, a bit,' I said with a sleepy smile.

'I have an idea. Why don't we get you into bed and I'll

read another sort of story to you; you can choose which one. Would you like that?' she offered.

'Oh yes, please, Ma,' I said, for I loved listening to her voice as she read to me.

'Thought you might have had enough of listening to someone reading today ...'

We both giggled a little at that, though later I really wished that she had questioned Michael and me a little more closely. Wouldn't she have asked herself why it was only me those two wanted to stay in the house alone with them? My two little brothers might have been too young, but Michael wasn't. Had he been questioned, my father most probably would have said he thought he was. What I realise now is that they wanted Ma to know about the visits and accept them as being good for her family. Which was most probably the reason Da began coming home with his unopened pay packet. Gone were the days when that small brown envelope went with him to the pub on payday, or so it seemed. At least that's what my mother began to believe – for a short time, she must have been thankful that all our lives were improving. Feeling that made her sing as she cooked and smile warmly at the priest on the Sundays when she was free to go to church. For wasn't it this priest who had made the miracle of her having a sober husband happen? And that was definitely enough to make him rise pretty high up in her estimation. Da had managed to convince her that it was all those Bible readings that had helped him turn the corner and become a better man, one who was determined to turn over a new leaf and become a more devout Christian.

I wonder how long it took for her to ask herself if there was not another reason for Father Pat's visits. Now, all these years later, I can't help but wonder when she came to realise what was taking place in her home when she was out working. Sadly, that's a question that can never be answered.

13

I can't remember if it was on the third or fourth visit when the mask slipped. That's when I finally saw the real person behind it. And seeing it, I had every right to be afraid.

The day had begun like any other. Ma had taken the two little ones over to Maureen's while Michael and I got ready for school. As soon as she returned, she got our breakfast ready. Da hadn't left for work by then so he, Michael and I sat down at the kitchen table as Ma passed over first some cereal and then bacon, fried eggs and for a treat, a piece of fried soda bread.

As I said, it was a normal start to the day. Well, that was until I had taken my first mouthful of food and heard what Da was casually announcing: 'Father Pat's coming over this afternoon.' Not one of us at the table, including him, would have known that he had just announced a visit that was to drastically change all of our lives. Even without knowing what lay ahead, hearing those words really spoilt my breakfast.

Father Pat arriving with Bible in hand meant that I

would be expected to come straight home from school. For some reason which I didn't understand until later, it was me my da wanted to be there when the priest visited. He was never going to agree to me going to a friend's house on my way back or making my way with Michael over to Maureen's. If he expected me to smile with pleasure and say, 'That's grand,' I didn't – I just felt it would be another day of being trapped in the house when outside the sun was shining and my friends would be tearing around playing.

I suppose with his black cassock and his sermons that seemed to please people so much that they waited outside the church to speak to him, it made me believe that Father Pat was quite important. Which was one of the reasons I still remained a little in awe of him. But important or not, I still found his visits boring – none of my friends were prayed over so frequently.

'Why's he coming again?' Ma wanted to know, something I too had wondered about but didn't dare ask. I just wished he wasn't. I just wanted to have fun with my friends, not sit in a stuffy parlour, listening to extracts from the Bible that made little sense to me and being asked to pray.

'He will be reading little extracts from the Bible and naturally we will pray together,' my father answered calmly.

Exactly what I had thought then. Hardly sounded like much fun, did it?

I knew what the prayers were about: Da becoming a better man. Given he had not stopped pawing me, I had my doubts about this. Maybe Ma was hopeful that these prayers were helping him to stop drinking so much. Not that his consumption of alcohol was ever mentioned – as in many homes, it was a taboo subject. So why should I have to stay in because of his foolish weaknesses? Angry thoughts were flashing through my mind. What was even worse was that he carried on telling Ma about what was planned after the priest had said all those prayers: 'And then we will sit, talk a little and once we have drunk some tea, he will answer any questions Gerri here is likely to want to put to him. He really admires her, especially as she is taking such an interest in these afternoons.'

Ma glanced over at me with a mischievous smile which told me she had a good idea what I was thinking. Somehow I stopped myself from giggling, managed to grin back at her instead and my anger and frustration dissipated. How I loved Ma – she worked so hard to make our lives better but still had time for our special moments together. Just a look could make me laugh and forget what was bothering me.

But the small hope I carried that Ma might tell us she would be able to return home early was dashed when she pointed out that she could not be back when Father Pat was here.

'Much as I would like to be,' she added.

'Oh, I know you would want to be with us,' Da replied laughingly. 'You're such a good woman,' he said, giving her a wink, which made her smile. 'You're not the one who needs to pray, are you? And my prayers need a little help, I think.'

'Just got to have a few words with your mother so you two get everything you need to take with you,' he added, turning to Michael and me. Catching each other's eyes, Michael and I slid off our chairs and picked up our school bags. My brother had already said to me, 'He's so boring.'

It seemed my father had no qualms about letting Ma see that he wanted to make sure I would come straight home. Just as Michael and I were going through the door he caught hold of my arm so he could have his final say: 'Remember it's you Father Pat seems to enjoy meeting, so when you get home, make sure you tidy yourself up and comb your hair. Understood?'

'Yes, Da,' I answered, understanding only too well that I was not going to have a fun day.

'Oh, and just in case I'm not back from work by then, you'd better keep an eye open in case he arrives before me. All right, Gerri?'

'Yes, Da.'

Not that I wanted to be on my own with the priest. He made me feel uncomfortable; he wasn't one of those grown-ups I could happily chat away to.

'Good girl,' he said, giving me a pat on the shoulder. 'Now off you go, you two.'

* * *

I couldn't help but feel a little resentful of Michael when we began walking to school. My brother was so lucky compared to me as he wasn't going to be stuck in the house when the priest came. He didn't even have to ask if he could go over the road to join his brothers and Maureen's sons.

After that first visit, when Michael could hardly wait to leave, he had just asked hopefully if he could go to Maureen's whenever he heard that there was another visit due that day. And Father's reply of 'Sure you can' told him there were no objections to him not being there. After a few more times he felt he didn't need to ask. Instead, as soon as he had dumped his school bag and swallowed a last bite of sandwich, he'd just say, 'Going off to Maureen's now' as the door slammed behind him.

All that day, niggling anxieties kept swirling in my head. Would my father be in the house when I returned from school? One part of me hoped he would be so that I would not be alone with the priest. On the other hand, it might be one of those times when he grabbed hold of me and ran his hands all over my body and did awful things to me. Those uncertainties might not have been so prominent, had I been told what time Father Pat was due. All I knew was that irrespective of whether Da was in or not, I was to be the one who had to let him in.

Now, as I look back on those weeks, I might have forgotten just how many times I had opened that door to him, seen the same smile, felt his hand on mine, but I'll never be able to erase the memory of every minute of that particular day and what occurred after he arrived. It's like having a video playing in my head, one that can't be turned off because it doesn't even have a pause button.

Often it starts to play just when I'm trying to drift off to sleep. Each film in that video series varies a little. Some nights my mother's in it and on those nights, it always plays the darkest parts of my childhood.

That's when standing in front of me is a little girl with dark blonde hair and huge blue eyes, looking bewildered and forlorn. She's in a small dismal room where a few family photos are hung on whitewashed stone walls. I can see a dark-rose-coloured settee, a couple of armchairs each side of a brick fireplace and a small cabinet, which my mother called her 'sideboard', where she kept her best china, glasses and a few other trinkets that were precious to her.

I know that if the door was opened, I would see something else: the bottles of Bushmills whiskey my father kept hidden in there. It was Ma who had tried to make it as homely as possible, using the little money she had left over each week, but however hard she had tried, it was still a stuffy little room; a room that over my last year in the house had become a place that made me shake every time I walked into it.

What had gone on in there managed to give both my younger and adult self almost-nightly terrors. I know the little girl who comes to me in my sleep is the ghost of my childhood. Every time she visits me, I want to reach my arms out to her and tell her that everything is going to turn out all right. I can feel her eyes searching my grown-up face for answers to all those questions my younger self posed. Such a vulnerable young child. That film of her standing in the parlour shows her confusion about what the priest had just told her, though it was not only that which disturbed her: it was also the expression in those cold, dark eyes of his. She had only just turned seven then. An age when a child is incapable of being able to articulate why she is suddenly frightened. But I know why that was. The priest's mask, which gave the impression of a kind, shy man, had slipped, showing the real person behind it. And who could she tell that to? She believed that the answer was no one. For hadn't she been convinced of that? So she did as she was told and kept silent.

The small child I once was had no understanding then that each of the priest's visits was to him a small but successful step towards him reaching his goal. Nor did she know then that her father, who she still loved, had neither the morality nor the guts to stop him. That was also something she found out that afternoon when she was in that room.

I hadn't needed to worry about my father not getting home before the priest arrived. There he was, freshly shaved and, for him, quite spruce. He was waiting for us in the kitchen and had already put a snack out for Michael and me.

I could tell by the way my skinny little brother sat down straight away and gulped down his food as fast as he could, that he was impatient to leave. It seemed he did not want to even say hello and goodbye to Father Patrick. Unlike most people in the village, he had already decided that he didn't like him.

'Why's that?' I asked when he confessed his dislike.

'He stinks.'

Well, there might have been a trace of aftershave scent, but I detected no other smell. But now I guess my brother just felt there was something bad festering inside the priest. Some adults and even more rarely a few children, I have learnt, instinctively sense the evil lurking inside a person; seeing right through the charm and the friendly warm smiles, down to the very darkness of their soul. Sadly, few have that ability, especially when the corruptor of small people holds a wriggling pup or a bag of sweets in front of them. Even if he wears the very mantel of holiness and respectability.

It was Michael, who many years later told me that he never forgot the priest and how he had hated being anywhere near him. Which is why that day is still etched on my mind, for as soon as he had finished eating, he took his satchel to the bedroom he shared with his brothers then sped off as fast as he could. All my father assumed was that he didn't want to listen to the Bible that he had made sure Michael had heard about. My brother might not have been interested, but it was Maureen that Da wanted to impress by hearing about it for wouldn't that show him in a good light and justify all the priest's visits?

It was not more than a few minutes after Michael left that the priest arrived. As usual it was me who was told to open the door to him, and as on previous visits, his greeting had not changed: he bent down slightly, took my hand and told me how pretty I was looking as he gave me the same smile as before. It made me feel even more awkward. The sun was shining and I wanted to be outside feeling its warmth, not making my way towards the parlour – 'It's the right place for us to pray,' I was told when I said it was too hot in there.

The first time he had said that, I must have looked at him with some surprise. Apart from Sundays when we went to church, I had never seen Da kneel and pray in the house, but obedient child as I was, I showed the priest into that humid room. He stood while Da and I got down on our knees on that hard floor. No little stools there, like the tapestry ones we had in church.

It was not until after the final prayer where Father Pat blessed all little children, that we were able to stand up. I'm sure I heard Da's knees creaking when we did.

'Would you like some tea now, Father?' he asked in a polite voice which I seldom heard used in the house. When the answer came in the affirmative, he told me to stay where I was and he would bring me in a cool drink and find some biscuits for all of us.

Once he was out of the room, Father Pat observed what a good man my da was – 'A wonderful soul, so full of goodness. Now, your da has told me a little about his feelings for you, Gerri. From the moment you were born, he saw you as being very special. I'm sure he's told you that as well, hasn't he?'

'Yes,' I muttered, my cheeks beginning to burn with shame.

'And you don't believe him, now do you? You just think you're ordinary, don't you?'

I said yes because I knew it was expected of me – I just wished Da would come in with our drinks as I was now feeling really uneasy. Father Pat sat with his hands on his knees, bending forward until my eyes met his as he repeated what a good man my da was and how he knew he did not commit sins.

I should have asked why he went to confession then but that question did not enter my head. Not with what the priest said next: 'He's done nothing wrong and nor have you, Gerri. You have to believe me there. He was right to tell you not to talk about what's happening between him and you because only a very few people would understand. Now it's me, not your da, telling you that; it's me, your priest. You are a gift from God who is so special and no one must find out. Because those who aren't special don't want children who are, near them.'

Another strong warning of why I should stay silent. One which I was naive enough to believe was my sake, not his or my father's.

It was then, as I was trying to take in what he had just told me, that he made his first move. The one he must have been waiting to make from the very first day we met. Compared to what he had in mind for later on, I suppose it was not as frightening as it could have been. It began with him telling me he needed to touch my body, that I was so full of love that he could feel my goodness coming from inside me. He then stood up, moved to where I was sitting and, placing his hands under my arms, pulled me gently from the chair. That didn't feel too frightening. But what he did next did. He knelt in front of me, the backs of my legs pressing against the chair, and I could feel his breath on my face. His hand was placed firmly on my shoulder, where it stayed for several minutes. It stopped me from moving sideways when his other one crept up under my skirt and continued right up until it reached my knickers. I could feel his long fingers touching that private part of me through the thin cotton fabric. I wanted to scream for him to leave me alone but I was frozen with fear. I could hear his breathing growing faster, but it must have been common sense that told him not to go further for it made him stop. Even so, for the small child I was then, it was just too much.

'Don't move,' he said as he wriggled his fingers around at the same time as he pulled me closer to him until my face was pressed against the lower part of his body. Now I could feel something hard under his black flowing cassock pressing against my cheek. I wanted so badly to squirm away, I remember thinking this had nothing to do with love. Love was the cuddles Ma gave me, love was the songs she sang and the tender words she used when she praised my drawings. I was still learning the difference between right and wrong, but surely this was wrong, even if he was a priest, for him to want to touch my body in my secret places?

Hadn't Da told me it was normal for him to do it, giving me the reasons and explaining why it had to be our secret? But he had never told me that other men could do the same to me.

That was the start of my childhood innocence leaving me. The confident little girl I had once been disappeared then to be replaced by one who was shadow-like, no longer wanting to be noticed.

15

Where was my da? That question was a silent scream in my head until finally, the priest let go of me. Relief flooded through me when Da walked in with mugs of tea and my glass of squash on a tray. I thought my ma would have been shocked that he was using chipped mugs and not her best china – it's funny how little things like that come into your thoughts when you are in shock.

I just wanted him to notice my expression, to ask me if I was all right. Couldn't he see how shaken I was? But apart from 'Here's your juice, Gerri,' not another word came in my direction. Looking back, I'm convinced he knew exactly what had taken place. Which must have been why he took much more time than was needed to make a couple of mugs of tea. I believed then, as I do now, that he and the priest must have planned that afternoon – Da would have been told to linger in the kitchen, giving Father Pat enough time to molest me.

As I tried, over and over again, to find understanding in how we had moved from kneeling and praying to this molestation, I looked at many alternatives. Something must have triggered that huge change in what happened when the priest visited, a belief that has stayed with me and still haunts my sleepless nights and insinuates itself into my dreams. What happened that day was the first memory that managed to seep through the barricade in my head, a barricade which up until then had stopped me dwelling too much on what my father did to me. Until then I still had the remains of my childhood love for him. It made me want to tell myself none of it was true when really, I knew it was. There is still, all these years later, so much grief in those memories. As they slowly return, tears rain down my face for days. I could be gardening or shopping in the supermarket. There are no obvious triggers, but suddenly the spectre is there, haunting me.

Although many years have passed since then, that afternoon is forever fixed in my mind. So, no, my father didn't ask what was the matter when he came into the room. And yes, he must have known there was something bothering me as I was sitting on a chair with my head down, staring at the floor. I suppose he knew what my answer would have been, so quite simply, he decided not to ask.

16

Now, as you are beginning to know my story, you might wonder why I hadn't got off that chair and walked out of the room. After all, there were excuses I could have used, such as 'I've got to feed the cat', or 'I need to go to the bathroom', but instead I stayed transfixed where I was. I just didn't have the emotional or physical strength left to draw my shoulders back, walk through the door and cross the road to Maureen's. Instead, still bewildered and shaken, I sipped my juice while I tried to ignore the two men sitting opposite me.

Once their mugs were drained, I heard my father mutter something about how he could do with another drink, only this time a proper one, and Father Pat saying so could he. It didn't take long for me to realise it was not more tea either of them had in mind.

'Right you are then,' I heard Da say as he just about leapt from his chair and went to the sideboard. He clearly didn't care if I saw what he was doing, for right in front of my eyes he bent down, pulled out a bottle of whiskey and two of Ma's crystal glasses. Alongside her white and gold dinner service, they were her pride and joy, only to be used when it was a special occasion like Christmas Eve or my father's birthday – a day she spent hours cooking all his favourite foods. I guess that Da thought it was a day worth celebrating for him and the priest. Even now, the thought makes me shudder at just how much lasting damage they did to my younger self.

That evening I was far too shaken up to feel any surprise at seeing that bottle being pulled from the sideboard. But then I really couldn't feel anything, I was so numb with shock. I knew Ma was coming home late that evening, as of course my father and the priest did too. I also knew that once Da started drinking, he would forget all about making my supper. He might have remembered he needed to do that if my brothers were there as well, but they would be well fed at Maureen's. I felt tears coming; it was not that I was hungry but now it seemed that Da just didn't care one iota about me. All I wanted was to get away from the two men, pick up Flo and take her up to my room and cuddle her and cry into her warm, soft fur.

Just when I was composed enough to move and began to wriggle slowly off the chair, Da looked firmly at me.

'Gerri, be a good girl and fetch your da a jug of water. Oh, and get yourself some more juice as well and if you fancy some biscuits for your tea, just help yourself.'

Him telling me to fetch things and bring them into the parlour made me realise that there was not much of a chance of me escaping from that room.

Poor Flo, she must have been waiting for me outside the closed door, for as soon as I came through, she busied herself rubbing against my legs. I bent down to stroke her and then, seeing her food dish was empty, I filled that and her water bowl. My father must have been getting impatient for he shouted through the door for me to hurry up. I don't know why, but for some reason it seemed that he didn't want to begin drinking until I was in the same room as they were. Not wanting his temper to change to his nasty one, which drink could often make worse, I filled the jug quickly, poured more squash and trotted back as quickly as I could.

Once I was back in the room he just about snatched the jug from my hands and nodded in the direction of the chair I had been sitting on, indicating I should sit down on it again. I guess he was itching to open the bottle but he didn't want to do so before I had brought in the water. For some reason he never, as far as I know, swallowed neat whiskey. Just a splash of water added told him what he wanted to hear: that he was not really an alcoholic.

I watched as his thick fingers slid over the top of the bottle, how quickly he unscrewed it. His eyes appeared almost closed as just for a few seconds he breathed in as deeply as he could to seize that quick rush of fumes released for the few seconds after a bottle is opened. His eyes lit up with anticipation as he slowly poured the golden liquid into the two glasses and passed one to the priest, who had pulled his chair nearer to the table in anticipation.

If I hadn't been in such a profound state of nerves,

I might have asked myself what he was doing here. I mean, if he was going to have a drink with a man who he was supposed to be helping to give up alcohol through prayer and support, what was the point of him visiting? But there was still some naivety left in the mind of my younger self. So I was completely unaware that it was she, not my da, who was the main attraction at our house for Father Pat. In the priest's eyes, my father was only a man who could help him put all his dark desires into action.

Until Father Pat had placed his tongue in my mouth and his hand up my skirt, it had never entered my head what the real reason for his visit was. Up until then I had believed he was a rather shy and earnest man. No one in our small town, myself and Ma included, suspected that his black robes and the Bible he was often seen holding presented a smokescreen that hid the truly evil person he was.

It was that knowledge that would completely unsettle me. I just didn't know what to do. It was when my father noticed that I had hardly spoken a word that he decided to get up and pour, as he said, 'a wee dram' into my squash. Maybe he thought the whiskey would take away my ability to remember everything that had happened, or that the next day he would be able to persuade me it had all been a bad dream or rather, a nightmare – 'Make you sleep a little better, darlin',' was all he said, giving my shoulder a little squeeze.

Might stop the feel of that flabby tongue of the priest in my mouth, more like it, I thought miserably. I could still almost taste the slimy long thing that had just about made me throw up. Not that I uttered a word to Da. He might have been trying to placate me, but that was not enough to stop me from being really angry with him. So, without any protests, I just let him pour that amber liquid into my drink.

'Come on, Gerri, now say cheers to us. That's what we do when we have a proper drink together.'

Cheers to who? Not you or Father Pat was the angry thought that came straight into my head. My mutinous side exposed, Da gave a small laugh as he grabbed hold of my arm and made my hand with the glass in it fly up in the air. Before I could put it down, I found myself looking straight into the priest's eyes. He and my father said cheers as they too raised their glasses. I was determined not to say the words and tightened my lips so that no sound could pass them. Young as I was, I felt not just angry and sick at what the priest had done to me, but also fed up with how I had been made to waste my time on all those other occasions, kneeling on that parlour floor to help Da give up the booze; all for no good reason.

For the very proof of that was sitting in front of me, sipping away at the drink that many women, including my mother, had named 'the ruination of our men'. Not that my disapproval of them drinking stopped me from also trying what was in my glass. Each sip I took of my well-doctored squash allowed some of my anger to dissipate and with each sip, the tension in my body slipped away. By the time my glass was empty I began to feel drowsy, my eyes drooping as sleep started to take over.

It was Da who shook me awake and got me up the stairs into the bathroom to brush my teeth and into bed. Then, he acted more as a father should, or so I thought. Now, on reflection, I know it was because he would hardly have wanted my mother to smell drink on me. Somehow he managed to get me into bed, pulled the bedclothes neatly over my small body and turned off the light. I must have fallen into a deep sleep for I never heard Ma come into my room as she always did when she came home from work. Sometimes in my sleep I sensed her presence and would wake, but not that night.

* * *

If my father had thought that the whiskey he had given me would make me forget the previous day, he was wrong. The moment I woke, I was nauseatingly aware of what had happened.

As pictures of that day flashed into my head, I was depressed and bewildered. I couldn't understand why Da, who I thought loved me, had done nothing to help me. But now I do. If there had been a club for men who wanted to molest innocent children both he and that priest would have rushed to become founding members. Instead, they had to make do with just two members and only one child to share between them.

One they had to use every trick in the book on to keep quiet.

Which I was for a very, very long time.

17

I did my best not to think about that visit when I woke the next morning. As I stumbled out of bed to get ready for school, I still felt a little woozy. Most probably I had a bit of a hangover, not that I would have recognised what that was at that time.

I made up my mind that I would ask my father not to leave me alone with the priest or let him touch me again. Silly me, thinking this strategy was going to work. But as he had told me so many times that he loved me, it was small wonder that I believed he would do as I asked. Once I had made that decision I began to feel a little better. Which made me able to carry on at school as though everything was fine at home. Or at least I tried to at any rate. I still wonder when Ma had worked out that there was something happening under her roof that was far from normal. I wish now I could ask her, for I still have questions in my head that I will never have the answers to.

Children certainly have a knack of seeing things that their parents believe they have successfully covered up.

I might have been a little girl, but that didn't stop me noticing how puffy Ma's eyes were and I just knew that something had made her unhappy enough to cry. There were evenings when, taking Flo with me, I had tucked myself into bed really early and fallen asleep listening to her soothing and rhythmic purring. Asleep or not, my ears and mind were tuned in to my mother's presence though she was seldom back before eight in the evening, having worked the whole day. The sound of her footsteps when she came into the house seemed to penetrate my sleep and, becoming half-awake, I would wait for her to come into my room. I must have been the child she wanted to check up on almost the moment when she returned. The child that I am fairly certain she was worried about.

Light from the top landing would float across my eye as she tiptoed in and sat on the edge of my bed. Wanting to touch her, my hand would reach out from under the bedclothes to hold hers, which made her smile tenderly down at me although even then I could see the sadness behind it.

I can now understand why she was unhappy. She had come back from a hard day's work, one with little joy in it, and as she came into her home she had to walk past a drunken husband before she could bring herself upstairs to check on her children. She must have been so desperately disappointed in him. I know that when he had appeared to be doing his best to stop drinking, she had seemed really uplifted and carefree. In fact, for a short time they had looked like a happy and contented married couple.

She must have felt the newly sober man he had been then was the same man she had married seven years earlier. Now he had disappeared again and she knew that there was nothing more she could do. Did she feel trapped? I think she did. And was she worried about her children? I'm sure she was. And was she becoming suspicious about what was happening under her roof when she wasn't there? I really do think so. But back then child abuse was not an openly discussed subject. It was taboo and incest was something so unholy that it was never, ever discussed so it was understandable really why the thought of it was hardly something she allowed to enter her mind. I think that she just felt there was nothing more that she could do to save her husband from himself.

But I was the one who knew exactly when Da's heavy drinking had begun again. It was when Father Pat had shown his true self to both of us. And since then, my father no longer bothered to hide who he really was when the priest was in our house. Just looking into those cold dark eyes that were focused on me with something that I now know to be lust made me shake with fear and caused my stomach to churn.

18

So, just how much of a hold did that priest have on my father? That I don't know but I think he had such a powerful grip that the only way Da thought he could escape from it was to pour as much Bushmills whiskey down his throat as possible. I still believe there must have been a small amount of goodness left in him and I suppose that made him depend on his friend, Bushmills, to escape his guilt. I could see the changes in him and I'm sure my mother did as well. When visitors were due, especially if it was Father Pat, my father had always shaved and put on a clean shirt after work – being an electrician was not a dust-free job. But after that visit he no longer bothered; he just walked around with a stubble-covered chin, bloodshot eyes and creased and dirty clothes which stank of sweat.

The only days Da looked smart, clean and hangover-free were Sundays, when we all went to church. He never made an excuse not to go, even if it was one of those days when Ma had to work. Those church services hold no good memories for me. Every one of those Sundays began the same way: helping to get my littlest brother who wouldn't stop wriggling washed and dressed, while I was already bilious at the thought of seeing Father Pat. Not only that, but I would have to sit still while the whole congregation looked almost spellbound, listening to him preach a sermon that I now knew was totally insincere. If that wasn't bad enough, mingling with people standing outside who were waiting to speak to the person they called 'the wonderful young priest' was even worse. They were lucky I didn't throw up on their shoes when their praise brought bile into my mouth. I just wished they could see the man he really was: the predator, the corruptor and the paedophile. But they only saw a shy young man with a kind, warm smile. A thoughtful man; one who, Bible in hand, visited the sick and the dying.

But that was not the man I saw.

I had seen him sneer.

I had seen him drink.

I had seen the coldness in his eyes.

So, no, those worshippers didn't have a clue as to who the real man was.

19

What I also found both peculiar and unsettling was that my father still went to confession. I suppose Father Pat had insisted on that, He must have wanted to hear as many sordid details as he could while he sat hidden in that holy confessional.

The father I had once thought so much of, right up until the priest assaulted me, seemed to have disappeared. I knew he had not tried to put a stop to the priest fondling my body. It seemed that he was enjoying the two of them indulging in their perverted games with me.

Ma might have just believed that Da had lapsed from being, as he said, dry. I am in no doubt that she fervently hoped that with the priest's help, her husband might just find the strength to stop drinking once again. Young as I might have been, I was the only one in the family who saw the weak side of him. Ma might have thought he no longer went to the pub to meet up with his friends because he was looking after me while she was at work but as I could have stayed over at Maureen's until she came back, I had other thoughts as to why that was.

Perhaps he was scared I would blurt out what was happening to me, or maybe his guilt was attacking him so hard, it was fuelling his depression. Whatever the reason, he chose to sit in that dreadful little room with a cigarette in one hand, a glass in the other and a whiskey bottle nearby so he could repeatedly top up.

Depressed or not, that did not stop him from allowing the priest to visit.

The next time Father Pat came, I was lulled into believing that my father would have told him to leave me alone. But I was wrong there, as I found out. It was about ten days later. And their practice runs with me had come to an end. They wanted more.

No, I'm not going to go into a huge amount of detail here about what happened during those visits that led up to his very last one. Nor can I bring myself to tell you everything that took place during that time. It's just too distressing for me to recount. But I will instead tell you about the horrific damage done to my small body, for that alone will explain what happened. Now you might ask how come, in a small school in an area where there was a strong community spirit, no one saw that there was something deeply wrong with me? Surely my brightness had visibly faded and I was depressed, if not beginning to be really ill?

The answer to that may be that what took place happened over a relatively short period of time. To begin with, I must admit, there was both physical discomfort and some considerable pain, though thankfully much of that remains a blur. The drink they gave me not only made me sleepy, it wiped out some of the detail of the sexual acts which took place. At least they were sensible enough to start to restrict their activities to a Friday when the school might not smell the alcohol on my breath. Also, they must have known that falling asleep in class might well have caused questions to be asked. Over the years I've learnt that children are more capable of hiding their feelings than most adults would expect. Especially when what was happening to me was so disgusting, I would have been far too ashamed to tell anyone. So, I did my very best to cover it up as, sadly, have so many other children who also keep silent about what they were told were 'secrets'.

I was pretty sure that the boys had not noticed much as they seemed to spend nearly all their spare time round at Maureen's so I was a bit surprised one day when Michael brought up the subject when we were coming back from school.

'I don't like being around Da when Ma's not there. He's so bad-tempered, isn't he? I bet he'll be in when we get back.'

'I suppose so,' was all I could manage, not mentioning how wary I was of Da and how him returning from work at the same time as us was making my life even worse. But there was more to come.

'Look, Gerri, can I ask you something? Is there something wrong with Ma? She's stopped singing. She always did when she was cooking or washing dishes. Have you noticed?'

He was right, she had, but I had just put it down to her being so exhausted.

'Well, Da's drinking again and he looks pretty miserable as well. And it's all happened since that priest began calling all the time. Maybe praying too much is getting him down? I mean, it's boring, isn't it?'

He was right about one thing: the priest's visits had changed the atmosphere in the house. But I knew it had little to do with holiness and praying.

20

I must have done pretty well at hiding mine, because the only person who ever asked me if there was anything wrong was Maureen.

'No,' I said quickly, when I noticed some concern on her face. 'It's just that I really miss having Ma in the house when I get back from school.'

'Of course you must, Gerri – I know how close you are to her. But you know you can always come over here when you get back from school, don't you?'

'Yes.'

'I don't know if your mother's told you yet, but from what she's said to me, she's certainly not planning on working those very long hours for much longer. She's spoken to Cathleen's daughter Rita about getting in more help. She didn't mind helping out to start with, but now she wants to spend more time with you and your brothers.'

Now that put a smile on my face. Seeing it, she gave me a hug.

'And Rita's coming over in a few weeks. She's taking

a holiday from work. So, your ma will be at home full-time for those weeks. Now, Gerri, doesn't that make you feel better?'

It certainly did. Realising that Ma being at home would mean no more visits from the priest and no more Da being able to maul me made me just about skip with joy. What I didn't say to Maureen was that for some time Ma had not been her usual cheerful self either. This was something else that had been bothering me. Nor had I mentioned to Ma or Maureen that I seldom saw Da without a drink in his hand these days. But we were brought up not to talk about private family matters to others.

From that moment, all the tension that was overwhelming me started to lift. Soon I wouldn't have to worry whether my father would be home or not when we got back from school. While the enormity of the difference it would make to my young life started to sink in, I felt my face breaking into the widest smile possible. One that made Maureen spontaneously reach down and hug me.

'There, Gerri! I knew how pleased you'd be,' she said warmly. 'And I'm happy for your mother too – I know she's missing being with you all.'

'Yes, I really miss her being in the house when I come home from school,' I said, not giving her the real reason why that was.

As I hadn't complained about being made to stay in the house with Da, or not liking the priest's visits, Maureen just thought that I needed my mother to spend more time with me. The boys might have been a happy bunch when

Da was around, but as she said to my Ma, 'in a household of males, a girl needs a mother who spends time with her.'

How do I know this? Because eventually, when I was a lot older, I reconnected with Maureen and she told me. Which is how I also heard that she had raised Da's drinking with Ma. Maureen believed it was very bad for a child to see one of their parents knocking back spirits any time, but especially during the day. She was right there, but what was far worse was that those two men put a small child's feet on the path leading to alcohol addiction when they forced me to swallow whiskey as well. As she told the adult me, back when I was a little girl, no one would have ever doubted a priest's integrity. It took many years before the media started to reveal the truth about the abuse that occurred within the Church. These accusations have appeared in newspapers, books and in documentaries on TV. Not every priest was a Man of God, it seemed.

So, Maureen hadn't said much at the time about Father Pat's presence in our house, especially as he was supposedly helping Da to stop drinking. She knew Ma didn't really want to talk about it and at that time neither woman knew that the priest himself was not averse to knocking back a few whiskeys. Neither of them would have thought for one second that Father Pat visited for any other reason than helping Da become a teetotaller. Maureen must have thought that straightening my father's resolve was surely a Herculean task for the new village priest, one that he was too decent to walk away from. Which meant that they still fervently believed that the priest was a good man. All she had said to Ma about his visits was that she didn't like the way I was expected to stay in the house when he was there – she just thought I was too young to be cooped up with the two men while they prayed.

'I never for one minute connected your depression to that man's visits,' she later told me, tears of remorse in her eyes. And I could tell that she still carried a huge burden of guilt about what finally happened. I could also see how choked up she became when she described how happy I had been when she had told me about my mother's change in working hours and how she planned to spend much more time at home. It was a memory that was painful for both of us – and for me it always will be. But she was right: I can still recall my happiness at the prospect of Ma being home to protect me.

* * *

I so clearly remember that evening when all of us had left Maureen's and gone home. No way could I let myself fall asleep before Ma returned, so I made myself comfy in bed to await her return. I had a book I could look at and Flo was curled up at my side. Like her, my ears pricked up at the slightest noise, because it was Ma's footsteps I was waiting to hear climbing the stairs.

When she finally walked into my bedroom and saw me sitting up in bed and smiling broadly, she must have guessed that Maureen had been talking to me. If she hadn't known, she did about thirty seconds later as I blurted out everything.

'Is it true, Ma?' I asked once I was able to draw breath.

'Ah, so Maureen told you all about Rita coming, did she? Yes, Gerri, it's true. I was going to tell you all in the morning.'

'I haven't told the others,' I said quickly, thinking maybe she had wanted to tell us all herself at breakfast. 'Maureen said it would be in a couple of weeks. Is that right, Ma? Will you be at home for our Easter holidays?'

'Actually, it's going to be sooner than I thought, darlin',' she said, lightly stroking my hair away from my face. Making herself a little more comfortable on the bottom of the bed, she did her best to explain a few things. She and Rita had hoped that Cathleen would recover a little more from the stroke, which was why Ma worked such long hours. Rita had been convinced that it might help her mother's recovery if she was seeing someone she knew so well every day. After talking to the doctors again, if was clear that there was going to be very little further improvement. Cathleen now needed more care than Ma could offer permanently, given she had four young children. Which was why Rita had managed to arrange time off work so she could spend enough time in Ireland to hire two new trusted carers and get them settled.

'She has good in-laws,' Ma said, smiling happily at me. 'They will stay with her husband and the grandchildren so Rita only has her mother to worry about for the time she's here. So, Gerri, the really good news is that I get to take two week's holiday and after that, I won't be doing all those long hours, fond of her as I am. I really want to spend more time with you and the boys. Only seeing you all for such a short time has made me miss you so much.' She paused to give me a kiss on the top of my head before hugging me tightly.

'Now what I was going to tell you in the morning is that Rita surprised me, because I thought she would not be coming so soon, but she's arriving in two days' time and then I'm having a complete break – and because of the hours I've put in, it's paid holiday!'

'In two days, Ma?'

I couldn't believe it.

'Yes, Gerri, in two days.'

She was laughing as she watched the joy spread across my face.

Talk about feeling excited! I could hardly concentrate on my lessons at school the next morning, I was just about counting the hours to when I would come back home and my mother would be there waiting for me. The priest wouldn't be visiting now and I wouldn't be left on my own with Da either.

Just two days to get through, I kept telling myself.

When I go back in time to those couple of days, I can see my younger self: a small blonde-haired child with flushed cheeks and sparkling blue eyes, skipping with joy alongside her brother after the news broke. I can hear their gleeful laughter as both children kept saying they could hardly wait for the two days to pass. Michael, always with an eye for the sweet things, kept saying our kitchen would be smelling of homemade cakes and biscuits again.

But when those joyous memories come into my head, other terrible ones follow in their wake. And I see that little girl with all her excitement and sense of anticipation, a mere twenty-four hours later. I now see a chalky-faced child, all blood drained from her cheeks, who is surrounded by an anxious medical team as she lies unconscious in an emergency ward, whirring machines attached to her tiny body.

And what was that team doing?

Watching her pulse and blood pressure readings and monitoring the machine that was helping her breathe. And praying for her not to die because of the extent of her injuries and the loss of blood.

21

Michael and I rushed back home so we could get changed out of our school clothes before both running over to Maureen's. I'm sure I was even more excited than him at the thought of the next time we would return home from school but then I had more reason to be, didn't I?

I can picture arriving back on that day so vividly. How my heart just dropped when I saw the one thing I had not wanted to: Pa's beaten-up old car outside the door. If only I had taken off and run straight over to Maureen's in my school uniform, all our lives would have been so different.

Maybe my father realised this was to be his last opportunity to have me to himself in the afternoons for he was determined to stop me running off to Maureen's when my brother and I got home. Perhaps he knew that it was Maureen who had spoken to Ma and told her that she was concerned: she had seen the changes in me and didn't think I was having a normal child's life. Although a devout Catholic, she had voiced her view that all that praying was not necessary for an innocent young child who should be out in the fields and playing with her friends.

I suspect once my mother had tucked me in that evening and seen that the boys were all sound asleep, she would have sat down and talked to Da about all the changes to our family routine. I don't know what his reaction might have been, but he certainly put on a very cheerful front when we all sat down for breakfast. When Ma told the boys about her being at home there were more beaming smiles from all three of them.

'It will be grand, won't it? Having your ma here when you two come back from school,' said Da, glancing over at Michael and me with one of his broad smiles. 'Bet you're looking forward to all that cooking and baking again, aren't you?'

Three small heads nodded. I must have been the only one who didn't think Da was as pleased as he seemed.

And I was right, as I found out when I came back from school. My father was both frustrated and angry. Ma would have thought that he would be delighted at being able to spend more time with his wife – he would surely be looking forward to having tasty meals put in front of him and all the washing and ironing done too? Perhaps it was the amount of whiskey he had already drunk that caused that black expression on his face. It seemed to me that it had drowned out all of the goodness in him.

By the speed at which the door opened, he must have stayed very close to it so that he could hear us arriving back. After all, he only had to glance at his watch to see how long he had to wait for us to return from school. The moment I saw him I knew straight away from the stern expression on his face that he had no intention of allowing me to go with Michael. So, what stopped me from turning, putting one foot in front of the other and backing away from the door? I was hovering on the edge of running off, but fear seemed to grip me.

'Off you go to Maureen's,' he said impatiently to Michael, who looked completely startled as he hadn't yet changed or had his usual snack.

'Is Father Pat coming then?'

At first he didn't get an answer, only a filthy look.

'He is. And he wants to see Gerri' As he said this, Da placed his hand firmly on my shoulder. 'So, you can tell Maureen she's not coming over this time. All right, Michael?'

My brother, who never wanted to be anywhere near the priest, just shrugged and began walking more slowly than usual towards Maureen's. By the set of his shoulders I felt that for once he was not completely happy about leaving me there. But then at six, he could hardly argue.

If Michael was not happy, I felt far worse. There was something about the way my shoulder was gripped that made me feel sick with dread. This was hardly the father I knew, the one who had given me Flo, teased me and walked on the beach with my youngest brother in his arms. That was the father I had loved for as long as I could remember. But that day it felt as though a completely different person had slid into his body and taken it over. Not only could I smell alcohol on his breath, I could sense his impatience and I knew he wanted to get me into the house as quickly as possible.

As I walked in, he quickly closed the door behind us. Maybe he still thought I might make a run for it.

'Now,' he said once we were both in the kitchen, 'there's your sandwich. Take it upstairs with you and tidy yourself up, Father Pat's coming over and your hair's a mess. And get out of those school clothes and put on that lovely blue dress that your ma made – you look very pretty in that. Now don't be wasting time up there, come down as soon as you're ready because Father Pat's due soon. And haven't I said this will be his last visit? Unless your ma wants him over, that is. You understand?'

'Yes.'

'Well, you be extra nice to him. You open the door and welcome him in.'

I could feel those treacherous tears beginning – I didn't want to be near Father Pat and I tried once more to make Da listen to me.

'Da, I don't want to. I hate him touching me. Can't I just stay in my room and take Flo up with me? You can just tell him that now Ma's going to be in the house from tomorrow, he won't be visiting again.'

I was confident Ma would not be inviting him to call.

I must have repeated 'please' over and over, until I could feel he was only seconds away from slapping me. He bent his knees so that his face was inches from mine and I could feel his breath on my face. As I looked into those eyes,

I couldn't see any love in them. I felt my courage drifting away. Somehow I managed to get out a question: 'Pa, have you told him not to touch me again?'

'I have. Now stop being so silly, Gerri. Run along and do what I've told you to do.'

'Won't you open the door to him then?' I pleaded and that was my final try.

'No, Gerri. Do as you're told!'

I was too frightened to stay where I was but filled with fear at what was going to happen later so I went to my room and did as I was told but not before my father had said that after prayers he was going to tell Father Pat about Ma being at home more. And that was the reason he had asked him over.

If only I had been a few years older I might have questioned why this was to be his last visit. Ma might not have invited the priest over herself, but she would have no objection to Da having him over – far from it. She wanted him to stop drinking. But then, as I now realise, that was not the reason he came.

The word 'prayers' should have raised a red flag. That meant going into the parlour and nothing good ever took place in there. I just had to listen to that priest chanting away, something nonsensical to me, and then watch as the whiskey bottle came out of the sideboard – a routine that I hated. A quick visit and some cups of tea would have made sense to my adult self, but not yet eight, I hadn't worked it all out.

So I did as Da had ordered me – brushed my hair and

changed into my pretty blue dress – but I felt too sick to eat my sandwich because there was such a premonition of danger running through my head. It was a warning, telling me that something bad was going to happen.

I really hated being near that priest. There was a feeling that he gave off. Did he think that he was above us, that he could do as he wished? And was I just a toy that he wanted to play with when he came through our front door? But what could I do? Refusing to open the door to him would only make Da angry and even if I dug my heels in, it wouldn't stop him from coming in, would it?

So, I did as I was told and opened the door as he knocked. And there was the sanctimonious priest with his Bible under his arm, smiling down at me. I had no choice but to let him take my hand and shake it, as he did every time he came.

'My, you're looking very pretty today, Gerri! Got all dolled up for me, have you?'

'No,' I said flatly.

'Oh well, you still look good,' he said blithely as he walked in and dipped his fingers in the holy water before leading the way into that nasty little room. Those prayers of his didn't take too long this time – they must have been in a hurry to get the whiskey out. I knew as soon as Da came back in, not with a glass but a jug of orange juice for me and another one with water that I was not mistaken in thinking that they would soon be drinking.

Out came the whiskey and I watched wide-eyed: it was the first time the priest poured it into their glasses. Then Da brought the bottle over to where I was sitting and poured just a 'wee dram' into my own glass of juice. It was when Father Pat lifted up his glass and said, 'Cheers to my last visit,' that I realised my father had lied to me.

So the priest already knew! So why was he here?

And that was when my unease began in earnest. I wanted to get out of that room so badly. As I was trying to think of an excuse that they would accept, I heard Da say, 'Come on, lift your glass up, Gerri! Show Father Pat here your good manners.' So I did. Glasses were lifted several times, before, on the third time of saying cheers, another 'wee dram' was poured into mine. It only took a few more sips of orange juice, by then well diluted with whiskey, to make me begin to feel drowsy. Clutching the arm of the settee, I managed to make myself sit upright.

Those two were knocking it back and I sat there with my eyes wanting to close. Squinting to see what they were doing, I watched as the priest poured more drinks and bleary-eyed or not, I noticed that more whiskey and less water went into Da's glass than it did into the priest's. I watched as they tossed down the drink and heard their laughter breaking although I had no idea what had been said to make them so amused. But when Father Pat turned his head around and I saw those large white teeth as he grinned at me, I guessed their laughter had been aimed at me.

'Can't have you falling asleep, Gerri, now can we?' he said as he got up and moved towards me. That memory is so very clear, despite all the alcohol and how long ago it was. It's as if I can feel every step he took towards me vibrating the floor under my feet. Was it then that I saw how his eyes glittered with excitement, or was it later that afternoon? My memory has played tricks with the sequence of events.

I know I was really frightened. Maybe if my father had been sober, he might have seen that there was danger in the air. Because I felt it was oozing from that man as he approached me.

That was when I tried to lift myself up from the settee and make a run to the door, but the amount of alcohol I must have consumed slowed me down and before I could stand, he grabbed hold of me and pulled me up so fast that I fell against his body. And then his hand flew up my skirt as it had done near every time he visited us. This time he didn't stop at the edge of my knickers, those long thin fingers of his went under them and pushed hard into my body; it hurt and I squealed with shock and pain.

Before I could scream at Da to stop him, the priest decided to stop me from making any sound. He tipped up my head, bent down towards me and his mouth fell onto mine, forcing it open to allow that thick tongue of his to slide down so far that I started to gag. The fingers of his other hand went up to my nose and pinched it hard so not only could I not cry out, I couldn't breathe. My whole body was quaking with fear by then.

'Now, be a good girl,' he whispered as his tongue and fingers left my mouth and nose. Gasping for air, I gulped it deep into my lungs. Tears were streaming down my face. He was not in the least bit concerned, I believe he was actually amused as his next gesture showed. His other hand went around my throat as he moved my small body backwards and forwards. Had I been capable of praying then, I would have prayed for my mother to come home. If only she was there, none of this would have been happening.

And then he stopped bouncing me about so quickly that I fell back onto the settee. By those wicked glittering eyes of his, I knew that more was to come. Not far off from losing consciousness, I could barely focus but managed to look up at Da when he finally stood in front of me. I thought he looked shocked.

He'll stop it now, I told myself.

He didn't.

Da was so drunk, he could hardly stand. Father Pat just looked at him coolly and said, 'You'd better give her another drink, that will quieten her.'

This time there was more whiskey than juice in my glass but I needed to get the taste of him out of my mouth and my throat hurt so much from being choked that I felt almost grateful when the soothing liquid slid down my throat. It made me even more sleepy and the two men seemed to retreat further away from my gaze.

'You get comfy now,' I heard Father Pat say as he pulled my legs up onto the settee and placed a cushion behind my head. I felt my skirt being pulled up, my father's hands moving all over me as I lay sobbing. The priest was pressing my shoulders down so I had to be still, but nothing was going to stop Da.

And no, I cannot describe what it was he did then. Please

don't ask. It's a memory I still find so painful that I cannot allow myself to speak it out loud. But I do remember how the priest's fingers on my shoulder grew tighter with excitement at what he was seeing.

I know I was sobbing uncontrollably when Da, with a grunt and a shudder, finished. I wanted to get off that couch and hit him with my small fists. I wanted to scream at him. But those wishes never stood a chance.

'Think it's my turn now,' I heard the priest say.

No!

I felt his hands slide under my body as he flipped me over. My face was pressed against the cushion. Another one was pushed under my stomach to raise my body a little. Thankfully all I can remember was a sudden and terrible red-hot pain that spread throughout my body before I blacked out.

Did I hear my father shouting?

I think I did. That's all I can remember.

So, I didn't hear the priest running out of the house. Nor did I hear my mother coming in. Or the phone call she made to Maureen to ask her to keep the boys for the night.

Nor did I feel her carrying me up to my bedroom.

But I do remember later, coming round and seeing her tear-stained face.

What I didn't know was that this would be the last time I ever saw her.

22

What else do I remember about that night? Even now there are some blanks in my memory, although over the years they have gradually come back to haunt me. Looking back, I now realise that I must have been drifting in and out of consciousness.

I have a dim recollection of a stranger standing by my bed at home. The pain must have gone away, although I'm certain that earlier on I had been screaming out with it. The stranger's soft hand was on my wrist, taking my pulse. Seeing my eyes flutter open a little, she said in a soft and reassuring voice, 'Gerri, you're going to be all right now.' And then the same voice told someone else, 'She's all right to go now.' Other voices in the background came and went. There was the sound of a woman sobbing that I could tell was Ma, for I had heard her cry before. I so wanted to say something to her, to stretch out my hand to hold hers, but I hadn't the strength. Then there was another voice, a man's, that I didn't recognise asking Ma, 'What has happened to your daughter? She reeks of alcohol! What in God's name has been happening here to give a child such injuries?' and Ma saying, her voice so choked up with tears, 'I don't know. I came back from work and found her like this and covered in blood and vomit. I just didn't know what to do and that's when I called you.'

As a comfortable blackness wrapped itself round me, the voices disappeared. The next thing I remember was the doctor's voice saying gently, 'Gerri, we're going to take you to a place where they will make you better.' Looking back at his choice of words, I think the doctor who had arrived with the ambulance crew did not want to use the word 'hospital' just then.

It must have taken all my mother's courage to have picked up the phone and described in pretty graphic detail the state I was in and what my suspected injuries were. She wanted to make sure that it was not just an ambulance crew that would come that night, that they would bring a doctor as well. But then Ma had been a nurse and knew just how serious my injuries were. And of course she had a medical kit she used, but that was at Cathleen's. Not that I know if there was anything in it she could have used that night to relieve my pain. Did the ambulance crew give me something? I suspect so.

Ma would have known just who was responsible for damaging me. It took me a long time to work out why she had kept quiet about naming them that night.

I must have come round slightly when I was lifted onto something flat (I later found out it was a stretcher) that began to slowly move as we moved out onto the landing. The man's voice was saying, 'Careful now,' when the stretcher was being carried down the stairs. The last thing I remember before being wheeled out of the house was Ma's lips on my forehand, giving me a kiss. Did she say 'Goodbye, my darling girl'? I think she did. Luckily, before the ambulance drove away, I sank back into a black fug of oblivion. Had they given me an injection or was the whiskey still making me drowsy?

Was Ma with me on that journey? No, she wasn't, I know that for definite now though for quite a long time I believed she was. Somehow she managed to enter my semi-conscious state. I felt her hand holding mine, heard her voice singing to me as the ambulance drove off with its blue lights flashing and the siren screaming shrilly, making any other traffic move over on the country lanes.

The whole village must have heard the sound, seen the blue lights through their curtains and wondered who had needed to be taken into hospital that night. Some would have crossed themselves and said a prayer. I know Maureen did. But then she was expecting it, I later learnt, although her intuitive sense of foreboding could never have predicted what was to happen later that night.

It can't have taken long for the rumours to start circulating – one thing I have learnt in life is that not all people who are supposed to not talk about what they have seen actually do. But that part of my story comes later. Then there's another vague memory of the stretcher being wheeled into a place where the lights were so bright that they hurt my eyes. My last memory is coming to a stop, the sound of curtains swishing shut and feeling a prick in my arm, which must have been an injection to completely sedate me.

I must have had doctors around me, assessing my injuries, before I was taken into the operating theatre. As far as I know, I was anaesthetised for many hours, judging by the scars I still have on my abdomen. I would have been in a recovery room afterwards, but I have no memory of coming round in there or being wheeled into Intensive Care rather than the children's ward.

So, what's the next thing I remember? Lying in bed, opening my eyes and seeing a woman dressed in blue and white sitting on the chair next to my bed.

Who was she?

I realised I was not at home but a place where white curtains were drawn all around my bed. It all seemed strange, for those curtains stopped me seeing any part of the room I was in. I was still far too drowsy to be worried about it but as soon as she saw that I was coming round, the woman sitting near me moved closer.

'Hello, Gerri,' she said, smiling.

I recall a round face with dimples and dark auburn hair pinned under something white. She was pretty, I thought, but who was she? Why was my mother not there? Or Maureen?

'Gerri, I'm a nurse,' she told me when she saw me looking puzzled. 'You came into the hospital last night. You've been little ill and I'm looking after you.'

Which was a very tactful understatement as I was eventually to find out that I had been in the theatre for a long time while they operated through my stomach to repair the internal damage to my bowel that had been done to me. When I glanced around through slightly unfocused eyes, I could see a tube attached to my arm.

'What's that?' I asked fearfully.

'Oh, just something to help you get better.'

She asked me if any part of me was hurting and I whispered with a tiny hoarse voice, 'My tummy. It feels funny and it's a little sore.'

'And are you thirsty, Gerri?'

'Yes.'

My mouth felt really dry. I could have gulped down all the cool water in a plastic cup she held to my lips while her hand went under my head and helped hold it up a little.

'Drink this – take sips, mind,' she told me, 'and you will feel a little better.'

It felt lovely as it trickled down my throat, but it tasted funny. Maybe there was some medicine in it, because I fell back to sleep pretty quickly.

The next time I saw anyone it was a man wearing a white coat with a stethoscope dangling around his neck. Not that I knew what it was then, I just remember that when he put it against my skin later it felt very cold. He told me he was a doctor and the poor man did his best to explain a little about the operation I had just gone through. Not an easy task for him, I'm sure – this was hardly a procedure normally performed on children. He did his best not to use too many medical terms and just said that they had gone through my stomach to fix me so that was why it might ache a little.

'And, Gerri, it won't take long for you to be fine again,' he added. 'You'll soon be running about outside.'

In fact, it would be several weeks before I was able to move around at all.

'Now,' he continued, 'we have to be careful about what you eat – just for a few days, that is. It will be a little bland, but you will soon be eating normal food.'

That explained what I had thought of as a sloppy mess that I was being given three times a day. The only operation I had heard any of the children at school having near the stomach was appendicitis so I asked if that was what it was.

'Eh, not exactly, but, well it was something like that,' was his embarrassed answer. He then told me he had to listen to my chest. Leaning forward, he placed the end of the stethoscope against it, while the other end went into his ear.

'You're doing just great,' he told me as he began to draw back the curtains around me.

'Where's Ma?' I asked before he could get out of earshot.

I'm certain I saw his shoulders stiffen before he turned round very slowly.

'She's not very well,' he said quickly, 'but nothing for you to worry about.'

'And Da?'

'Oh, he's looking after her, so he'll be coming soon.'

Not that I was told what 'soon' meant.

* * *

I don't know how long I had been in that hospital before I had a visitor, who once again was someone I didn't know. She introduced herself as Marion and she said that she had heard I wasn't very well so she had brought me some books to read.

'Thank you,' was all I could say although I was curious as to who she was. What she didn't tell me was that she was either from social services or the police and had come to see if she could get any information out of me. Surely she would have known that the nurses would have tried asking me questions once I was able to sit up? They were as gentle and tactful with their questions as they could be, but had given up when it was clear that I could not remember.

Marion must have known that, but that did not stop her asking me, 'Did you have some sort of accident before you came into hospital, Gerri?'

'I don't know' was all I could say and I wished she would go away.

'Well, I've heard that before you were brought here you were in a lot of pain. Don't you remember that?'

'No, but my stomach hurt when I woke up.'

'And who has come to see you?'

I can just see my younger self now, propped up in bed, the youngest patient in the IC ward, being asked such tactless questions. That last question reduced me to tears. Because no one had come. Not that many visitors were allowed on that special ward. Marion had only been allowed in to see me after showing the duty nurse her credentials. And she was bringing me some books. I must say she was got rid of very quickly. It took less than thirty seconds for the ward sister to walk quickly over and say I needed to rest and must not be upset.

Another thing I can remember really clearly are those blanket baths, as the nurses told me they were called, that I had every day. They were so careful when with a soft flannel, they gently washed me down, taking great care to avoid all the dressings on my stomach. Talk about every bit of me being squeaky clean. It was when they washed me the first time after my operation that I saw the mass of bandages that seemed to cover so much of my body that I became frightened. *What was underneath?* The nurses, when they saw me flinching, were very kind and covered them quickly. When the dressings needed changing, it was done under some sort of cover so that I could not see what was underneath.

Had I been an adult, I suppose I would have known what to expect. A doctor would have talked the patient through the operation in all its stages. But how could those doctors and nurses explain such a large wound to a frightened small child? A child who could not remember what had happened to her. Although I suspect they too believed it was merciful she couldn't. Because something dreadful must have happened to cause her injury.

As I look back on that time when my younger self was

both scared and lonely I now know it was merciful that those memories of what had happened that night were blanked out. It was as though nature told the brain to push them away until she was strong enough to bear it. Though I don't think she ever was. For when gradually those memories came back my younger self, I really wished they hadn't. To say she wept would have been a gross and tragic understatement. It nearly broke her. And it took a long time before she could come to terms with what had happened not just to her, but to all of her family.

23

The nurses in the ICU went out of their way to spend time with me although they were so busy monitoring the other patients. They knew that I would have to be told the reason why my mother was not visiting me. The decision had been taken for me not to be told the truth until I was fully recovered: I would be too frail to receive such heartbreaking news and it could cause a serious relapse.

It was bad enough that I was both sad and lonely, but I was also becoming suspicious of all the excuses about why no one was visiting me and that was beginning to do me more harm than good psychologically. The nurses were aware of that, which also made them concerned about how moving me onto a ward where visitors were allowed would affect me. ICU did not have a precise visiting time, which meant I had not seen a stream of visitors coming in, just the occasional anxious wife or husband, mother, father, brother or sister who would only be allowed to stay for a few minutes. But once I was moved to another ward, I would certainly be exposed to family visits.

Which would make everything far worse. In the end, the hospital social worker contacted both my father and Maureen. Da agreed to visit me over the weekend when he wasn't working, Maureen said she would come almost straight away.

Years later, she explained to me why it had taken her so long to visit me. She said it was never because she didn't want to see me; in fact, just the opposite. It was the telling of lies she was going to find difficult. She is such an open person and the thought of also having to keep looking cheerful when I asked about my mother was going to be more than difficult. For she too was grieving Ma, who had been her closest friend. On top of that, she was having to cope with my three brothers, who so far only knew that their mother had been taken to hospital. Sooner or later, they too would have to know the truth. Which of course should have been their father's duty, but more on that later.

Maureen was really dismayed when she heard how depressed I had become, which was why she agreed to come straight away. And as in the children's ward we could wear our own clothes, she had the painful task of going into the house across the road to pack a few things for me.

Before I went to my new ward, the nurses told me it would not be long before I was walking about, once my stitches were removed. I'm sure they were dreading having to do that. For if the sight of the bandages had upset me, goodness knows how I was going to react when I saw that huge wound dissecting my small frame. Oh, they made a few jokes to try and make me giggle. Like how I was so prettily stitched up by the doctors that maybe they did embroidery as a hobby. But still, pretty or not, those stitches now had to go.

'And then if the doctor is happy with everything, you'll be able to walk around a little,' they told me. As I was still bedbound, not only did the nurses have to wash me, but they also had to help me onto a bed pan; that odd-looking cold metal thing that I managed to perch on to relieve myself. And then when I was done, it was taken away. I did feel a little peculiar when I was sitting on it, knowing that they were waiting for me to finish peeing (which smarted a little) so that they could take it away and get it washed and put away.

I can still vividly remember the day those stitches came out. My younger self might have been brave, but nowhere near brave enough to stop herself wailing with fright when she saw that vast wound, for there is no other word for the puckered vivid red scar running up the centre of her stomach. The wound was swollen and the stitches seemed too tight to hold it together. If they took them out, would it burst open? Would it bleed? For there was dried blood on the stitches so would fresh red blood gush out when those thick black threads were pulled out?

I was frantic with fear; I must have thought that I had been nearly cut in two. I remember that the nurse had to give me something to calm me down. That day I was in a state of shock and just about lost it. Wails and screams would hardly have a good effect on the other desperately ill patients in the ward so they waited for the sedative to do its work and only then did they start snipping at the threads.

By that time, I was one very miserable little girl. I still didn't know what had happened to me. All I knew was that I was in hospital and was missing my family just about every single minute of the day. I missed my kitten Flo too. 'Where are they?' I kept asking. By then I wanted my mother so desperately, I needed to feel her arms giving me hugs and hear her reassuring voice singing into my ears. I kept asking the questions that the nurses were forbidden from answering.

If Ma was ill, like that doctor had said, then where was Da and where was Maureen? I had always been confident that she loved me as well. I know the nurses and doctors went out of their way to be kind but that did not compensate for me being left alone and feeling abandoned. And that was when the dark cloak of depression wrapped itself around me. I was beginning to think that no one loved me. No one; if Ma was ill, why had my father or my brothers not come to see me? It was as though I was dead to them.

Even though the nurses kept telling me I would be happier in the new ward as there were a few children of my age there, it made little difference to my plummeting morale. It wasn't strangers I wanted, it was my family. I can't really remember the move to the new ward but I can vividly recall the first visiting time. There I was, sitting up on my bed, staring hopefully at the open ward doors, watching visitors streaming in. I felt my heart just about jump with joy when Maureen walked in with Michael by her side. She was all warm smiles and gentle hugs, warning my brother not to hug too tight and hurt me. Before she even sat down she was full of apologies about not coming sooner. She told me she had so wanted to, but her hands were rather full with all the children staying in her house.

'Where's Da then?' I asked bluntly.

'Oh, between looking after your ma and working, he's very busy, darlin'. But he sent his love and he's planning to come soon.'

The idea of a visit from my father excited me. Just when I was about to release a stream of questions, all of which were bottled up inside me, Michael, unusually shy, moved from her side to give me a gentle hug as well. Somehow I felt he didn't look the same boy that he was the last time I saw him. A distant memory came to me then: him walking off to Maureen's and leaving me with Da. I tried to force my mind to give me some more clarity, but it refused to let any more detail in at that point. What I could see though was that Michael's cheeky grin was not there anymore and not only that, he looked tired. I asked them about our other two brothers, who I was missing too.

'Couldn't they have come as well?'

For a second Maureen looked uneasy.

'Oh, the little ones are too young really. They don't allow very small children on the wards. Peter also has a bit of a cold, wouldn't be very popular if we gave that to all the patients.'

No sooner had she made those excuses than she quickly changed the subject: 'As you'll be walking around next time I see you, thought I'd better bring you over something to wear from home, your own nightdress too,' she said, placing a bag in my locker. When that was done, she managed to divert my attention by pulling out from another bag the presents she had brought for me: a selection of fruit, some colouring books and ones for reading, a pack of crayons and lastly the doll that had always stayed in Ma's bedroom – I had always loved that doll.

'She wants you to have it,' Maureen said when she saw how much it seemed to mean to me, though she didn't explain why. With her arm around Michael and her hand holding mine, she told me what I later concluded was a piece of complete fabrication. I suppose there was some smattering of truth in it, but not a great deal.

'The doctors here think that when you are ready to leave hospital, it would be better for you to go to a place where you will be well looked after. They've said that in their opinion, you will get better faster there. It's all been arranged, but there's a little good news: Michael will be going with you so that you won't be lonely.'

I didn't think any of that was good news.

'Why can't I go home? I mean, Ma's a nurse,' I said.

Maureen, probably expecting that question, had the answer well rehearsed. She quickly told me it was because I would need some special care for a while – 'Plus, you don't want to fall too behind with school, now do you?'

'No.'

'Well, there's teachers there so both of you will be having lessons.'

'And Michael's really coming with me?'

'Yes, he is.'

The next question I asked was about Flo: who was looking after her?

'She's staying with us until everything's sorted,' was her reply. Hearing that, I caught Michael's eye.

'She's all right, Gerri, she likes being with all of us. She has plenty to eat and she keeps bringing in dead mice to give to Maureen. She thinks it's a present,' he said with a faint impression of his cheeky grin.

I had to giggle at that; I felt a little relieved too, for I could tell by his expression that he was telling the truth. I felt the warm fingers of my brother's hand, sliding over mine.

'Don't worry, Gerri. I really will be coming with you.'

And then a bell rang, signalling visiting time was over and they had to leave.

* * *

Still nothing had explained where Ma was. It was when I was lying in bed in the early morning, my eyes shut but my ears open, that I heard two of the nurses, who must have thought I was still sleeping, whispering to each other.

'It's so sad what's happened to her.'

'Poor little girl, it's so awful.'

'And who's going to tell her?'

'I don't know.'

But when I opened my eyes and asked what it was I needed to be told, they just said I had heard it wrong. It wasn't me they were talking about. But I didn't believe them. And why had one of them blushed? You only did that when you were caught lying, didn't you?

24

It was years later when Maureen told me that it had been agreed between the hospital social worker, Maureen and the head of the home that Michael and I were going to that I would be told about Ma once they had me settled in there. They all agreed that it was for my own good that I did not find out how she had died.

Maureen had offered to be the one who broke the news. The others thought that with all the questions I might fire at her, she would find it too difficult so they said no and the principal of the home told me. When Maureen and I met again, I had known for a very long time.

I had suppressed so much of what I had gone through, but there was a lot of grief and fear in the hospital, exacerbated by not understanding why Ma or Pa weren't visiting. And that was to be made worse by my father's final act. Later, the staff at the home would try to help me through the horror of learning the truth and why I was sent away. It was much later that I was told more of the reason why I could not return to the village: it was because of the scandal that would sweep through the place, and the vile and nasty rumours. That I had slept with my father was one obvious one. But the main reason was my mother's suicide, which to that tight Catholic community had to be the greatest sin of all. It was so great a one that she could not be buried in the consecrated grounds of the church. And knowing about scandals and how destructive they can be, Ma had made sure her children would leave the village forever.

25

Whereas my brain had been foggy a lot of the time in the ICU, once I was moved to the children's ward, I am sure I became more alert. I suspect that I had been given medication to keep my memories at bay as much as to deaden the pain. There were now other children that I could talk to and then there was the challenge that one of the nurses had given me.

'I bet you a packet of your favourite sweets that you'll be walking in two days.'

Sounded good to me and I was certain I could do it.

Almost as soon as I had sat on the bed pan, hopefully for the last time, and finished my scrambled eggs on toast, two nurses came to my bedside. One of them said, 'It's walking time today, Gerri,' The pair of them placed their hands under my arms so they could help me slide out of bed. I felt really shocked when my legs, as though they were made of rubber, buckled beneath me as soon as I tried to stand.

'What's wrong with them?' I asked, panicked.

'Nothing, Gerri. Don't be scared,' one of them told me

very calmly, 'it's just that you've been in bed for a long time and they're out of practice. They'll soon be working again, you'll see. Now let's try again. We'll hold you up.'

After a few tries I managed to stand, although I swayed a bit when they released their hold of me for a minute.

'Good girl, now put your right foot in front of your other foot. Don't worry, we've got hold of you, we won't let you fall.'

I tried, but those legs of mine let me down and my knees buckled again. But I wasn't going to stop. *I'm not a cry baby*, I told myself, doing my best to push one foot forward again. *Nothing like a little determination*, I thought when a few minutes later I managed a tottering few steps. Even if the nurses had been supporting me, it didn't stop me feeling very pleased with myself.

'Well done, Gerri,' both nurses said.

Even though it brought back memories of my baby brothers learning to walk, I felt a wide smile of satisfaction coming onto my face.

* * *

As I had been told, there were others around my age on the ward and I was able to chat to them. One had a broken leg, another tonsillitis and two were in for appendicitis and proudly showed me their neat stitches on the tiny incisions. I kept my scar covered up, for I knew no one had a huge wound like me and I still hadn't totally grasped why it was there.

At least I began to feel less lonely on that ward. Each day I made myself walk a bit more until I no longer needed any help. So it was goodbye to bed pans and blanket baths, though I still hated seeing that ugly scar when the dressing was changed. There was still some gunk coming out of the wound so the dressing remained on and I was told I could have a quick shower as long as it didn't get too wet.

It was the visiting hours that really got me down. All the other children were sitting up in bed with an excited look of anticipation on their faces, while there was me peering hopefully at the doors, just wishing and wishing it would be my mother and not theirs walking through them.

But it never was.

26

'Your da is coming to see you on Saturday,' one of my 'walking' nurses told me with a wide smile. She looked almost as happy about it as I was. 'Good thing you're walking well now, isn't it? He's going to be so proud that you've managed it so quickly, isn't he?'

I whispered a yes, although I had my doubts.

It was then that she sat down in a chair next to my bed and was joined by another lady, who was introduced as the social worker for the hospital. I faintly remembered her visiting me before in ICU. She was an older lady and seemed very kind. It was she who gently asked me a question: 'Gerri, can you remember now what happened just before you came by ambulance into the hospital?'

'No,' I whispered, for my memory still seemed blank and that frightened me a little.

'Well, what's the last thing you remember before you came in here?'

'Ma singing to me in the ambulance.'

There was a pause for a second while she quickly thought of another question.

'And the last thing you remember before the ambulance came to your house?'

'Coming home from school with my brother Michael.'

'Tell me about it.'

I could feel my forehead furrow as I tried to picture it. It was as if a mist had cloaked my memory and I really struggled to find the images I was looking for.

'We were happy,' I said finally.

'Why?'

'Because Ma was going to be at home more.'

'Had she been away from home a lot then?'

'Not all the time, it's when she was looking after the old lady, Cathleen.'

'Was your mother upset about anything that you can remember?'

'No! She was happy too; she wanted to be with us more.'

'Do you remember if you fell on anything?'

'No. Where's Ma?' I asked plaintively. Just hearing the word 'mother' had triggered the tears slowly running down my face.

'Oh, Gerri, I didn't mean to upset you,' she said, noticing my tears.

'Where is she?' I persisted before bursting into loud hiccupping sobs. But not before I saw her eyes catching those of the nurse, which again made me feel that they knew something.

The nurse who I now knew quite well got up and sat on

my bed. She put her arms round me and my head rested on her shoulder as her hand stroked my back rhythmically. For the first time since the hug from Maureen, I felt a little bit comforted. I could have sat there like that for ages and she seemed to sense that. Slowly my sobs settled and only the occasional hiccup remained.

27

It was those two nurses who I had formed a special bond with, who on seeing how upset I was, decided to buy me a present: a new dress so I could look really nice when my father arrived. They placed a package in my hands saying, 'It's a reward for being so brave, Gerri. A little present from us both to a plucky little girl who learned to walk again.'

I was so excited, I could hardly get my words of thanks out. Inside the package was a pretty yellow and white dress which made me gasp with joy.

'Yellow and white are happy colours, aren't they?' one of them said, stroking my hair. 'We'll get that washed and shiny as well for you.'

Now, when I look back all these years later and think of that day, a lump comes into my throat. My younger self so wanted to look her best. She thought just maybe, if she looked pretty and healthy, her father might decide she could go home instead of sending her to that place she had been told about. She was so excited that he was finally coming to see her and having a new dress and freshly washed hair was going to make the day perfect. The nurses had also added a yellow and white bow to her hair. She wanted him to see that she could walk and was much better. They had helped her lift up her arms so that the yellow dress would slide down her body.

'Don't you look pretty?' both the nurses said when I managed to twirl round.

There was a big clock on the wall. When the nurses left me sitting on my bed, I watched its hands jerk forward as I counted the minutes to when the doors would open and visitors would be allowed into the ward. I watched as smiling couples bearing gifts came in to visit their children. But my father wasn't among them.

Maybe he's just a little late, I kept telling myself.

But he didn't come.

So, I sat there and refused to move until visitors' hour had come to an end. One by one, they all left. Then I climbed into bed, still wearing my pretty yellow dress and clutching my pillow for comfort. I curled my small body up as tightly as I could and cried. One of the nurses came over, a worried look on her face, but I just turned away.

I would never see my father again.

28

I have only a few recollections of that momentous day when Michael and I were taken to the home. I can remember that I needed a new dressing on that livid, puckered wound of mine. It was something I hated seeing, so I tried to look up at the ceiling instead of looking down but when the nurse removed the old dressing, I couldn't help but glance because I was curious to see if it had healed any more. Seeing the still slightly soiled dressing told me little progress had been made.

'Why is it still leaking?' I asked with a hint of desperation in my voice.

'Oh, you mustn't worry about that,' the nurse told me. 'The hospital wouldn't let you leave if they thought it wasn't getting better. And it is, Gerri – trust me, it won't be long before you won't need a dressing.'

'Will it look better then?'

'Of course it will, my love. It just takes a little while, that's all. Soon you won't even notice it.'

I have to say I must have been told that to cheer me up

a little because that scar has never faded away. True, it is not so discoloured and puckered but I will carry it with me to the grave as a constant reminder of the harm inflicted on my tiny frame.

I can remember Maureen, with Michael just behind her, walking into the ward, all smiles and hugs. How happy I was to see them and just for a few moments I hoped maybe this time she had agreed to take me back to her house. I guess when she saw that hopeful expression on my face, she must have realised what was going through my head and quickly made sure I understood that was not going to happen.

'I've decided to be the one who takes you to the new place, where you two will be well looked after. You'll feel a lot stronger in no time at all, Gerri.'

I tried to hide my disappointment and squaring my shoulders a little, I gave her a hug. Before I could say a word, she told me she had bought a few more things for me to wear – 'Come and take a look,' she said as she began pulling them out of the same bag that had presents in it the time before when she visited me.

There were a few pairs of pretty bikini knickers – 'Can't have the elastic rubbing on your scar until it's completely healed, which ordinary ones will do. And here's a couple of nightdresses, which will be more comfortable for you than pyjamas,' she said, holding them up. I can still see the pattern on the fabric: small bright yellow ducklings on one and the other was blue and white stripes. Funny how we can remember pieces of clothing but forget other things.

'And here's something for you too, Michael ...'

A lovely royal blue sweater was given to him. Now that made his face light up as blue was his best colour.

'You two can see I've been busy knitting. I only just finished yours last night, Gerri,' she told me as she pulled out the last item in the bag, a really beautiful cardigan in my favourite shade of deep pink. I certainly managed a big smile then. 'Now, we'd better get everything packed up – I can see your locker is just about bulging,' she added.

Maureen had also brought a small suitcase with her so that we could pack everything that was in my locker as well as her presents and the dress the nurses had given me.

'Right, we're just about ready to go! Gerri, I expect you have a few goodbyes to say, haven't you?'

I had, but I was beginning to feel miserable. I had been in the hospital for so long, I felt almost scared of what might be waiting for me outside. It would have been all right if it was Maureen's house we were going to because that was familiar, but I had no idea what the new place I was going to would be like. Would the people there be as kind to us as the nurses had been to me? And the children there that I had been told about, would they be friendly to a couple of new people? And the last big question was, who would visit us there?

I had a horrible sinking feeling then that we were being got rid of. Our father clearly no longer wanted us around and where was Ma? Not a question I was brave enough to ask. Glancing at Michael, he looked none too happy either. I doubt he wanted to leave the comfort of

Maureen's house for some place he had never heard of, just to keep me company. It meant he was leaving his brothers and everyone he knew behind. To be fair, he did try to put on a brave face but then Michael had always been a plucky little boy.

'At least I'm looking forward to having some lessons again,' he said, 'aren't you, Gerri?'

'Well, yes, I suppose so,' I said, feeling rather puzzled. I had been given a few exercise books in the hospital, ones where I could write answers to questions but I hadn't really thought of school that much. I knew the summer holidays had come to an end so surely my brother had been back in the classroom?

'Haven't you been going to school, Michael?' I asked, wondering if he had been unwell too.

'Erm, no. Our teacher was off sick.'

Something wasn't quite right but now was not the time to bring it up.

Maureen was already holding the bag and suitcase so I knew it was time to go. As we began to move forward, the nurses who had been the jolly ones who changed my dressing and the ones who had got me to walk came over to hug me goodbye. They told me the place I was going to would make me even better and gave Maureen a bag of dressings for whoever would be doing them in the future.

I know I was miserable that day, for no matter what reasons I had been given, I wanted to go home. And that scar was bothering me. But like Michael, I managed to put on a brave face and thanked everyone for looking after me.

And then we were out of the hospital and into the car, with our baggage in the boot alongside a suitcase of Michael's things that was already in the car.

It was then that I asked Maureen where all the children were, my brothers and her sons. I think she told me their grandparents were there.

Meaning theirs, not mine.

Not that I remember ever having met mine. Which I had been wondering about for some time. I mean, why had I never met them? That was another question I was going to ask Ma. But I had left it too late, hadn't I? In the end I didn't get an explanation for several years.

29

All I can remember about the drive was the sound of the windscreen wipers. Within minutes of us setting off, dark grey clouds had burst open, letting sheets of rain pour down, blurring all the colours of the countryside.

We passed low stone walls behind which beady-eyed sheep stared at us. There is something about blustery rainy days that makes us feel gloomy so Maureen turned on the radio and fiddled around, trying to find some music that would cheer us all up. I don't think there was much conversation in the car. Really, what was there to talk about? And as for the multitude of questions that were in my head, I would never really get satisfactory answers.

I expect I had drifted off a little into a world of my own before I heard Maureen announce cheerfully, 'We're almost there now.' She made it sound as though we were going on a holiday, not to a home for unwanted children. Still, I peered out of the window, trying to see as much as I could as she drove down one of Ireland's many narrow and unkempt country roads. At the end, we came to a high brick wall that hid the grounds behind it from view.

'We're here,' she told us as she pulled up by a wooden gate. It was the type that normally sits between a road and a field. Maureen told us to stay in the car and she jumped out to open the gate. As we drove up the pitted drive, I saw a large grey stone house that looked pretty old.

The door opened even before Maureen had a chance to ring the bell and we saw a young woman, who with her dark hair tied up in a ponytail, was dressed in jeans and a red T-shirt. She looked young and friendly and gave us all a welcoming smile.

'You must be Mrs Doyle,' she said, 'Matron's expecting you. Best get in and out of the rain quickly,' and she stepped aside so we could all walk in. 'Let me give you a hand with their cases,' she offered as she picked one up from the doorstep and introduced herself as Jessica. 'And I know who you two are. You're Gerri and Michael, aren't you? I've been looking forward to meeting you and so have some of the children here. They were quite excited when I told them that you were coming.' And another warm smile came in our direction.

'Come along, I'll take you to Matron's office – she's expecting all of you for tea. While you're with her, I'll take your cases down to the dormitories and we can sort them out later after Matron has shown you around. And then lunch will be ready. All right?'

'Yes,' Michael and I both said.

I really liked Jessica straight away, which removed one

of my worries about whether the staff would be as kind as the nurses.

Following her down the corridor to the Matron's office, I could hear children's voices coming through a door. They sounded happy as they called out to each other and that cheered me up as well.

Even though I wish I was at home, at least this place doesn't seem too bad, I thought.

When we arrived at the matron's door, Jessica gave a gentle knock before opening it. My first impression was that it looked more like a cosy sitting room than an office. The woman who greeted us was older, most probably in her forties – certainly no ponytails or jeans for her. Instead, her rather stocky frame was dressed in a navy-blue suit, her dark hair streaked with grey pulled back into a tight chignon. Still, her welcoming smile seemed friendly enough when she told us to take a seat.

'You must all be a little thirsty, so tea and orange juice are on the way. Now let me run through the rules of the house.'

The drinks were brought in and Mrs McNally, as we learnt was her name even though she was called Matron, explained that we must never leave the grounds without permission. Everything else sounded pretty reasonable. It was more about where we would have our lessons, meal and bath times, and how there was to be no talking after the lights were out. How much Michael and I took in, I'm not sure.

'Well, I'd better show you round now,' she said, getting

up from behind her desk. 'I expect you'd like to see where they will be staying before you leave?' she asked Maureen.

'Yes, I would. Thank you, Matron.'

So back into the corridor we all went and the first door the matron opened was the one where I had heard children laughing – 'The playroom,' she told us. Which I could see was a really large one. There were a few children in there who were about the same age as Michael and a couple of older ones who were playing a game with toy cars with younger ones. One boy – Freddy, I was to learn – toddling around on plump little legs reminded me of my youngest brother Keith. It made me think just how much I was missing my family, but before I could get tearful, Mrs McNally told the group that Michael and I were coming to stay and we received more smiles and offers for us to join them.

'After lunch they can,' Matron said as she ushered us out.

Through the windows of the small classroom we went to next, I could see that the grounds outside were quite extensive. The matron, noticing me peering out, told us there was more space at the back of the house: 'We keep chickens there, so there are always plenty of fresh eggs and parts of the grounds have been turned into a vegetable garden. There's an established orchard too, so lots of apples, pears and plums on the menu when they're in season. Cook makes jams and preserves too so we use everything we grow.'

After we had glanced through the doors of the dining room, we went to the dormitories. There was one for boys, another for girls and the matron pointed out which were to be our beds; our cases were standing next to them. There were the same kind of lockers that were in the hospital, only these were just a little bigger and were made of wood, not metal. We were told that this was where we would place our clothes but there was a place downstairs where our coats and outdoor shoes were left. She then showed us the boys' and girls' bathrooms, which had several washbasins and shower cubicles. And that concluded the tour.

What we hadn't been told was that the children in the home were not expected to be there for long. Part of Matron's job was to do her best to get them adopted or even fostered. Ma must have known that when she had decided this was the place she wanted Michael and me to go to. In the letter she left behind asking for us to be taken there, she had only one request: Michael and I were to be kept together. Da had to sign his agreement to her stipulations, which he did. Then again, I didn't know about the letter or what made my father agree to its terms until eight years later.

After we had seen everything there was to see, Matron and Maureen shook hands and Mrs McNally discreetly walked away, giving us time to say our goodbyes. Maureen hugged us both and said she was really impressed with the place and felt confident that we would be happy there. Did I see tears forming in her eyes as she straightened up and turned to go? I'm sure I did.

Michael and I stood on the top step forlornly, hands entwined for comfort, as we watched the car drive off with the one person we knew cared for us. My stomach lurched – we had been left in a place full of strangers. It was then that I heard Ma's voice whispering in my ear, *They won't be strangers for long, Gerri. Some will become your friends. This is a good place for both of you. Maureen's a good friend and you will see her again.*

And I did, but not for another nine years, at the age of sixteen.

30

Looking back, I don't know if it was just exhaustion or a cloud of depression that swept through my body on the first day at the home – I suspect it was a generous dollop of both. Physically my body had been through a lot and so much had changed for the worse in my life. I can tell you that Michael and I felt very downcast as we watched Maureen's car disappear from sight.

It was as though we had just seen the last of everything that was familiar vanish. Neither of us knew what the future held. Realising it was now just us two left together, questions which had been in my head for weeks swam to the surface. Already I had worked out that Michael didn't have the answers but I just knew that Maureen did. I couldn't understand why she wouldn't tell us what was happening – all we knew was that we had seen neither of our parents for a long time.

I hadn't had time to tell my brother about the day my father had upset me so much. But I did later that day at the home after I had taken an afternoon nap. Michael came up to the dormitory to see if I was awake. He perched on the end of my bed and I told him how the nurses had washed my hair so that it was all shiny and clean. I got dressed in my new dress and then I sat for hours with my eyes glued to the door of that hospital ward, waiting for a father who never came.

'He never even rang to say why,' I told him. 'Not even a letter or a card with some sort of excuse came later. Did you see Da when you were at Maureen's?'

'No, Gerri. Maureen can't stand him. I know she went over to see him once and that's when she brought Flo back and that's as much as I know,' he told me.

'But our house is just over the road from Maureen's. Didn't you go over to see what was happening?'

'I knew Ma wasn't there. Maureen told me she'd been ill and had been taken away to a place where she could get better. So, no, I didn't go over – I didn't want to see him. The last time I did was when he was holding your arm to stop you coming to Maureen's with me and you looked frightened. He's a bully, Gerri. He made Ma's life miserable a lot of the time too. I'm sure it was him who made her ill.'

It was then that he asked the question that had been going through my own mind too: 'Do you think we're ever going to see our family again, or is it just going to be us now?'

'I don't know, Michael, I really wish I did,' I told him sadly.

Ma loved us, didn't she? She wouldn't forget about us.

I knew that, or so I kept telling myself for the next ten days. The eleventh day was the one when Matron decided I was well enough to be told the truth.

I suppose the decision not to tell us that our mother had died on the night I went into hospital was taken for a good reason. No one knew how long I would take to recover or how much harm knowing what had happened might do to my recovery. But I think now we would have been better off if we had been told earlier. It was not just not seeing Ma that was upsetting us, it was being kept away from our brothers and not knowing what was going to happen to us.

Michael and I were both hurting badly when we stood on those steps as Maureen vanished from view. So much had already disappeared from our lives and now it seemed that she had also gone. Both of us had noticed that she had not mentioned coming back to the home to see us, nor was taking us out for the day mentioned. I had hoped that she might tell us something about Ma – where she was and how she was. But Maureen had managed not to mention anything about her. I knew by the bleak expression on my brother's face that he too had hoped Maureen would have told us more.

Just as Michael and I walked back into the house, Jessica appeared at our sides, cheerfully saying she would take us back to our dormitories to help us unpack. I'm sure she must have been waiting nearby for us to say our goodbyes.

As neither Michael nor I had that much in our cases, it would not take long for our belongings to be placed in our lockers. Jessica took us to the dormitory where I would be sleeping first. Although I had been allocated a bed, I noticed a couple of other empty beds in the room. She told me to choose the one I wanted.

'The one by the window,' I said.

'Great, now let's get all your belongings in the locker,' she told me as taking them out of the case, she showed me how to fold everything neatly – 'Don't want to get creases in your pretty dresses, do you?' I watched how she lightly folded and placed them in the locker with great care.

Next, we went to the boys' dormitory, where she showed Michael, as she had me, the best way to pack his clothes in a locker.

'Now, I'll take you to where you can hang your coats.'

And back downstairs we went to a deep alcove next to the back door, which led to the orchard and vegetable patches.

'See, you already have your names on your pegs. And this is where you leave your outside shoes too. Got to keep the floors clean,' Jessica told us with a grin. 'Now, lunch – I should think you two are feeling a bit hungry by now, aren't you?'

'I am,' Michael replied quickly and then I remembered that for someone so skinny, he didn't half eat a lot.

'And you, Gerri, how's your appetite?' Jessica asked.

I managed to say that I was hungry too, even though I had far too many butterflies fluttering away inside my stomach. She gave me a rather piercing look then and asked if I was all right because she thought I was looking rather pale.

'My stomach's a bit sore,' I told her.

'Do you feel well enough to have your lunch with the others?'

I managed to nod my head.

'Seems to me you need an afternoon nap after lunch. You've only just come out of hospital and the journey here was quite long. Maybe I've had you walking around too.' Then her hand caught hold of mine. 'You're going to be fine after a couple of days here, everyone is nervous when they first arrive. After lunch I'll have a look at that dressing of yours when we get back to the dorm.'

I smiled up at her then. Resting suddenly sounded good to me.

'Right, let's get you both into the dining room – I know I want something to eat as well.'

Still holding my hand, she pushed open the door and in we went.

I might have told her I was all right going into the dining room for lunch, but the moment that door swung open those butterflies fluttered a lot faster. Walking into a room where I knew no one was not something I had done before. I mean, I had lived in a village where we knew just about everyone. And as for the children in our class when I started school, I had known them ever since their mothers had wheeled our prams together so none of us were shy with each other. Not having met more than a couple of the girls in the home when we were being shown around, I wondered nervously what sort of questions the children there might be asking: wouldn't they want to know why we were here? And then I began to wonder why they were there as well.

Inside the dining room was one long table and another smaller one with baby seats on it for the toddlers and the younger children. A girl of about eighteen who seemed to be in charge was sitting with them as she helped the littlest ones spoon some food up. Jessica walked us over to the long table, where I could feel several pairs of eyes fixed curiously on us. Not that I needed to worry for as soon as she introduced us there were lots of friendly hellos. One boy moved up so that Michael and I could sit together. They told us their names, not that I could remember them all straight away, and although they looked a little curious, they must have known better than to ask many questions. In fact, they seemed more interested in what we liked doing rather than why we were there.

I felt more relaxed with all the friendly chatter around me and the food was a lot tastier than what I had been given in hospital. A couple of mouthfuls and my appetite seemed to miraculously return. And no, I can't remember exactly what it was we were given – fish pie, I think. I know by the time I had nearly finished it, I could feel my eyes beginning to droop.

Michael seemed to have already made a friend – Tom, a red-haired, freckly-faced little boy, who was sitting opposite him. The girl sitting to my left-hand side, who had the dark hair and blue eyes of a true Irish child, told me her name was Holly and that she was in the bed next to me.

'See you chose the one next to the window,' she noted.

'Yes, there were a couple of empty ones and Jessica said I could choose. I really like looking out of the window in the morning when I wake up.'

I didn't ask her how old she was, but I guessed she was two years older than me. She asked me questions about whether I liked reading, explaining that she did. And then she asked another question, which I didn't understand.

'Are you looking forward to Sunday?'

I asked if she meant that we would be taken to church on Sunday morning. It was not one of my favourite things, but I thought it would be better not to say that.

'Well, church is good too, but I meant in the afternoon. You know, when we dress in our best clothes and wait for those visitors to come.'

Seeing the puzzled look on my face, she tried to change the subject but one of the others, hearing her, chipped in with a little more information: 'It's when people come to look at us and we're all sitting there in our best clothes, wondering who will go this time.'

'You mean your visitor?'

'No, they're everyone's visitors. We know what they want – they want to choose which girl or boy will go and live with them.'

I began to understand though not completely, but more or less: they wanted to give some of us a new home. That made me feel uneasy, because all I wanted was to go back to mine.

31

It was only when I finally got to meet up with Maureen all those years later that I found out that she had known Mrs McNally (as she called Matron) before we went into the home. And it was also a revelation to learn that she had kept in touch with her over the whole time Michael and I stayed there. Discovering these facts shed light on a lot of Matron's actions during our stay.

'When you two went there, she had already been running that home for nearly ten years,' Maureen told me. 'She didn't want you meeting those Sunday visitors before she had been able to sit you down and tell you both about your mother's death.'

She went on to explain that Matron might have been a pragmatic woman who believed in being forthright straight away, but like it or not, she had to listen to the doctors and they had stated she wasn't to say anything to us, especially not telling us that our father had already signed the papers to agree to our adoption.

Matron had told Maureen that it was 'bad enough to

know about her mother's death but finding out that none of the children were wanted by the father would be too much for her to handle'. Maureen had to admit that this was probably sound medical advice.

As we sat together, she explained that Matron just prayed that she would find a kind, caring couple, who would take both Michael and me into their home. People who would, over time, give us enough love and affection to help us come to terms with our past. She knew how difficult it was going to be to break the news that, until she found the right couple, we had no home to go back to.

'Those who organised the adoption of babies have a much easier task,' Maureen added as she went on to explain something I had already discovered – that trying to find a good home for small children with a loveless or cruel past was seldom easy: 'By the time she met you and your brother, there was little she hadn't seen.' Maureen told me that over those ten years a great many children had come through the doors of the home, all of them had different stories and none were happy ones. Certainly quite a few of those children had been mentally damaged during their early years, which made Matron feel it was important to make them feel as secure as possible once they were in her care. She always insisted on being informed of the reasons they were sent to her; she was also aware that however hard she tried, not all of them would end up having happy lives. What really distressed her at the beginning of her career was when she believed she had found a good home for a child, only to have them returned. Oh, there were many different excuses such as 'she wets the bed', 'he plays with himself' and even 'my husband and I can't stand the screaming when he or she has those terrible nightmares'. Being returned to the home caused even more damage to the child. It certainly made them feel that they were unwanted by everyone and cringe away from those Sunday visitors.

It was then that Matron came up with the idea that the children would only be told that they had been invited somewhere for a weekend. In fact, she suggested to those who were interested in adopting a small child that they visited at least twice to see how they all got on.

'Which I know now didn't work for you, Gerri.'

'No, it didn't,' I agreed.

Not that I wanted to talk about that part of my life then; it was not something that I found easy.

Maureen went on to tell me a little more about Matron and her role: 'She had to deal with those frightened and bewildered children who had been removed from their homes because of undisputedly cruel treatment. She might not have shown it but seeing those scars that cigarette burns had left on small, malnourished bodies made her feel sick and angry. There were even a few who had never been sent to school. And one who you personally knew, Gerri, who had been rescued because a neighbour became suspicious on hearing a child's screams. It was the abruptness of the scream stopping that convinced the neighbour that a hard hand had been placed over the child's mouth, which resulted in a phone call to the police.'

'Yes, that was Holly,' I said. 'She told me about it while

I was there. She was lucky though, her uncle who lived in England found out where she was and managed to take her into his and his wife's home. And I'm lucky to have her as a friend. I also know there were those who had lost a parent or even two when Ireland was at its peak of the Troubles.'

Maureen told me that Matron had just hoped none of those memories were still lodged in their brains – 'But she did say that she had never seen a child who had been so damaged physically and mentally as you had been. What monster had done that to you was the question she wanted answered. Of course, she asked me if I knew.'

'And you did, didn't you?'

'I was fairly certain but I was also aware of why your mother didn't want it proved – she knew just what a scandal it would cause. Which was one of the reasons she made sure that all of you were removed from the village; she just didn't want the story following you.'

According to Maureen, Matron believed it must have been my father who had committed such a vile act but without any evidence and a child who had lost all memory of that night, which for my sanity at the time was a blessing, it also meant that nothing could be reported to the police.

*   *   *

It was when I had been in the home for about ten days that another suspicion surfaced, one that both shocked and concerned Matron – not that she dared do anything about it. Matron knew that with suicide being a heinous crime in the Catholic faith, my brothers and I would have suffered a great deal from hearing all the scandalous talk surrounding our mother. She made sure before we came that no one who worked there had any knowledge of what had happened. Trying to stop me and Michael from hearing too much about the visitors until the doctors had given me another examination would hardly have been easy for her either. As she couldn't prevent the children in the home from talking about them, she decided that it would be easier to arrange a day out for us on our first Sunday, which she did.

32

So, although Michael and I kept hearing about all those afternoon teas where groups of visitors came to meet the children, we did our best to ignore the conversations. We could see that some of the children were excited because they so badly wanted to find a nice family to go to. Their dream was to have their own bedroom, a puppy or a kitten, new clothes and be taken out to all different kinds of places, the seaside being the most popular one. We were not that curious because we had a home with Ma and Pa, didn't we? One day we would be going back to it. All I had to do was get better, wasn't it? That's what we tried to convince ourselves every time we were on our own together.

I think now that deep down, both of us knew that our parents had given us up. Even so, we found it hard to believe that Ma wouldn't want us any longer. Hadn't she sat at the table and told us how much she was looking forward to spending more time with us? And hadn't she kissed the top of my head when I went to bed and hadn't she been singing 'Funny Face', my favourite song? Which she only did when she was happy – so much for good old Irish tunes! Neither of us could think of a reason why she would have changed her mind, we kept telling ourselves. So, we did our best to push those other thoughts away.

Not that it stopped us talking about it when we were alone in the garden. The question that kept coming up was, where were they? To us it seemed like a lifetime since we had seen our family and neither of us had done anything wrong, had we? We talked about our brothers too and wished that Maureen would bring them over for a visit. I can remember all these years later just how unhappy and confused Michael and I were then.

Seeing our despondent faces, Matron came over and told us about her plan for Sunday. I think we must have brightened up a little when she told us it was Jessica who was going to take us out for the day and even better, as far as we were concerned, it was on a Sunday. Jessica was going to drive us out to somewhere she knew, where we could have a picnic. Matron told us that she thought the walk to church was too long for me and that a lie-in would do me good. She then turned to Michael to say he could of course attend church if he wished.

'I know you're fit enough, Michael, but I thought you might want to go with your sister, so it's up to you.'

'Think I ought to stay with Gerri, Matron,' he replied with one of his rare grins.

I'm sure that Matron knew dangling a treat like going for a picnic and getting out of going to church was something my brother was not going to argue with. Church had never been his favourite place and going on a picnic sounded much more fun. I was pretty sure I could have walked there, but a lie-in and a picnic were far more tempting.

Luckily, we weren't mature enough to figure out that Jessica's act of kindness was to ensure we would not be there when the visitors arrived. After all, as she and Matron both had cars, I could easily have been driven to church. I think she had asked Holly to be a bit discreet about asking how come we were going out for the day when all the others were going to church as usual. All she said when she saw that I was not getting up and dressing for church like the other girls was, 'Lucky you, enjoy yourself,' with a warm smile.

33

A morning lie-in was a real treat and very different from the time when I had to spend whole days in bed when I was in the hospital. Back then, it was the 6 a.m. sound of bedpans rattling on a trolley that woke me, instead of the chatter of the other girls in our dormitory.

As I opened my eyes, I observed that each one of them had already got their Sunday outfits of pleated dark skirts and light woollen jumpers on. They kept turning around to ask each other if they looked all right and then they took their berets out of their lockers.

'We don't have to put them on until after we have had breakfast,' Holly told me as she swirled hers around on her finger. 'Mind you, Jessica has the job of making sure we're all tidy and neat before we leave,' she told me just as Jessica popped her head round the door.

'Morning, Gerri,' she called out. 'You just stay where you are and rest until I come back.'

As Holly left the dorm to go to breakfast she said, 'And you have a nice day out and I'll see you later.'

Jessica came back just when I was telling myself that I had better get up and pull some clothes on.

'Right, Gerri! Everyone except your brother is making their way to church now. He told me he fancied some nice scrambled eggs which our chickens have given us and then toast with honey. Now, does that sound good to you?'

'It does,' I agreed – I was wondering if I was going to get breakfast if I missed the communal one.

'I think these are the clothes most suitable for sitting outside when we have our picnic,' Jessica told me as she pulled the pink cardigan that Maureen had knitted for me and a light woollen dress from my locker. 'Michael's already up and about.'

'Of course he is,' I said, smiling. 'Bet he got dressed as fast as he could when you told him you were making us a special breakfast. It's a wonder he didn't go down with the others so he could have had two of them, isn't it?'

Jessica laughed and said, 'Yes, I've noticed that he likes his food.'

When we went down, Michael was already there waiting for us: 'Morning, sis,' he said as I gave him a pat on the back while Jessica scuttled off to the kitchen to make our breakfasts. I must say we both wolfed it down when it was placed in front of us – 'Best breakfast we've had for a long time,' I told her. Then I wished I hadn't as it brought a picture into my head of Ma standing at the stove, chattering away to us as she busied herself making pancakes for our breakfast on the last day I saw her.

Jessica, who seemed to spot just about every little thing,

must have guessed why my eyes suddenly sparkled with tears and quickly said, 'Now that you've finished, let's get our picnic into the car. I can't wait to set off! We're going to one of my favourite places and I think you're going to love it there as well. And look, the sun's shining, so it's a perfect day for us, isn't it?'

Both Michael and I agreed with her, for we were country children, who were used to being outside even in the middle of a frosty winter. So, picnicking on a sunny autumn day would not have bothered us one bit.

We took our plates back to the kitchen and then put on our outdoor shoes and picked up our coats before we went out to where Jessica's shiny red car, which she told us was a Ford, was parked.

'Chose this one because it runs well on bumpy roads and there's definitely plenty of them around here,' she said as she opened the boot so our coats and the picnic basket could be placed inside. Michael and I climbed into the back seat and off we went, down the rutted drive down to the gate.

When Jessica jumped out to open the gate, I felt a little lump in my throat. It was only a few days since Maureen had done the same. Michael caught my eye and as his hand slid over to clasp mine, I could see the same thought had occurred to him too. I realised then that however chirpy he tried to be, he too felt sad that she seemed to have disappeared from our lives.

You must push that to the back of your mind, a voice that I felt sure was Ma's whispered in my ear. Or was it just my imagination? I wasn't altogether sure, but it made me sit up straight anyhow.

Jessica chattered away to us as she drove along the country lanes, where fields that had been golden just a few weeks ago were now bare of crops. The farmers had let the cattle graze in them and I knew once the stubble was demolished, bales of hay would be put out to feed them over the winter. In other fields sheep and cows munched on bright green grass for already the autumn rain had started.

We came to another gate and this time it was me who jumped out to open and close it.

'We're here,' Jessica told us as she drove up what seemed like a well-maintained driveway leading to a large redbrick modern farmhouse.

'Who lives here?' we asked in unison.

'It's my uncle's farm,' she told us, looking over her shoulder at us with a grin. 'He breeds horses, you'll see them when we get out of the car. I phoned him before we left and he said he's a bit busy so we're to look around and go where I like to picnic, and he'll come over later. So first, we'll have a bit of a wander. There's a new foal in the field behind the house; I expect you'd like to see that?'

Michael and I both nodded eagerly.

'Right then, I've brought some carrots with me – horses like them,' she told us as we all got out of the car. 'So, let's go and put our stuff down where we'll picnic and then we'll go and see the horses before we dive into our basket of food.'

Both Michael and I thought Jessica was great. We could

hardly believe that she'd not only arranged a visit to a special farm like this but also cooked our breakfast and prepared more food for a picnic.

When we walked to the fields behind the house, we saw several horses in a field with white wooden fences.

'Those are the elderly ones,' Jessica explained, 'they used to be racing horses, but my uncle has given a home to some of the ones that have retired.'

Jessica gave us some carrot chunks to give to the horses – 'Just hold your hand out flat,' she told me as I approached a beautiful black horse who had trotted up to the fence. As I did as she instructed, a silky mouth brushed against my outstretched palm and gobbled the carrot chunks greedily.

Just as we moved to go to the next field, a couple of black and white collies came bounding over to Jessica, who knelt and stroked them. Not far behind them came a tall man whose trousers were tucked into green wellington boots and who had a tweed cap covering his head.

'Hello, niece,' he called out as he walked over to us.

His burly arm went around Jessica as he gave her a hug then he turned to us and said, 'Nice to meet you both,' with a warm and welcoming smile. 'My niece will be showing you round and here you go, Jessica, this is for you three,' he said, handing over a large paper package. 'Your aunt's out, but she baked some cakes yesterday that she thought you would all enjoy.'

He was right about that for they were simply mouthwatering when we ate them later.

'Now, would you two like to see my foal? She's the latest one to be born here.'

'Yes, please,' we chorused (while Michael and I had seen lambs and calves, we had never seen foals before).

When we got to the field where a light chestnut mare and her creamy coloured foal were, I just thought they were beautiful. Jessica's uncle, seeing my expression, gave a single piercing whistle – enough for the mare and her long-legged foal to come trotting over to the fence. Lumps of sugar came out of his pocket and I watched in fascination as they took them from his hand. Seeing them so close was the best part of that day – it made me forget nearly everything that was troubling me.

We walked around a little more, looking at all the contented horses before returning to our picnic place. Jessica asked her uncle to join us, but he declined, not before telling us to enjoy our lunch. Taking his two dogs with him, he walked back to the house as he'd told us he had some calls to make.

When we had finished eating the chicken drumsticks, salad, slices of homemade cake and apples, we all walked up to the farmhouse to say thank you for having us. Jessica's Uncle Harry, as I learnt his name was, said that we were welcome to come back any time. Then it was back to the car as Jessica drove us back to the home. To my relief, the visitors had all gone when we arrived back. There was some chatter about them when we had supper, but I was much too full of my day out to listen intently – that really was the best day Michael and I had experienced for ages.

34

I wasn't to know that Matron had decided that she would have to sit Michael and me down the following Monday and give us the terrible news – news that would leave a gaping hole in our lives for many years. I'm convinced now that under her pragmatic mask was someone who was dreading what she had to tell us. Not that she showed any of those feelings when that Friday she told me that the doctor had told her that my scar had healed nicely. Well, the doctor might have decreed that, but I felt like saying as far as I was concerned, there was nothing nice about having such an ugly, puckered scar. I'm sure she knew how I felt about it, for she changed the subject quite quickly: 'You'll be pleased to hear that Jessica has offered to take you and Michael back to the farm again this weekend. So, another picnic for you two, although it will be after church this time.

'It's quite a pretty walk to get there – it takes about fifteen minutes – and the doctor has approved you doing it. In fact, he said it would be good for you. And the other bit of good news is that you can now treat yourself to a proper bath. I expect you'll enjoy having one after all this time, won't you, Gerri?'

I found myself smiling at her as I said, 'Yes, I will.' In fact, I could hardly wait to have the whole of myself immersed in soapy warm water instead of trying to wash at the basin.

Bath time for us all was every Saturday night, after we had our evening meal. It meant that we would wake up on a Sunday morning all bright and clean. The little ones were taken care of in another room where Marie, the young woman I had seen with them on my first day, looked after them.

When I told Holly that I would be joining the other girls for a bath she said, 'I'll race you there, see who gets there first!' Well, she did – being nimbler on her feet she had shot up the stairs and got there first. Running up behind her, I managed to be second in the queue.

There were only five girls in our age group who were also getting ready for their baths. We all got undressed and then queued up in our bath towels, waiting our turn. I soon realised this was not going to be the long soak I had longed for. If I had thought that we just got into the warm water and bathed ourselves, I was mistaken. A plump middle-aged woman who we called Auntie Paula was supervising our baths. She used to tell us stories about her daughters when they had been the age we were then – 'And now they're all grown up, with their children about your age. I love it when they come to visit and I get time to play with my grandchildren – we grannies love spending time with them all.'

A sentence that, as soon as it came rather tactlessly out of her mouth, made her look embarrassed. After all, not one of us had grandparents who loved us enough to take us into their homes.

'Anyhow, now I've got you lot to take care of,' she added, 'so today is called "Lets Get You Squeaky Clean Day.'

Holly could hardly have been in there more than five minutes before she came out wrapped in her bath towel, saying with a grin, 'Now it's your turn, Gerri! She's a bit generous with that soap. I've got to get my hair dry and that seems to take forever.'

She was right about the soap – my whole body must have been lathered with it, including my neck and face. Some of it even went up my nose and made me sneeze. I know it was carbolic soap, because I can still smell it today and it's as though a piece of it has never left me. I can also remember those strong fingers of Auntie Paula's when she wanted to make sure our hair was as clean as our well-scrubbed bodies. Once she was satisfied that she had finished with my limbs, she used a metal jug to scoop up water which was poured onto my head before a big dollop of shampoo landed there. It seemed those strong fingers of hers were also determined to make sure that every hair on my head was clean. Then when she was satisfied that she had done enough, I had to duck my head down into the bathwater to rinse it before I was free to clamber out.

The plug was quickly removed as the grimy water ran out to be replaced by clean before the next girl was called in.

It's funny really when I look back at those late Saturday afternoons. There we were, all between eight and ten, sitting around in our bath towels, laughing and chattering as we rubbed away at our hair. It sounds more like a teenagers' night in when I try and describe it, instead of a group of little girls trying to dry their hair. To us back then, we found those bath nights fun. And we were all children who needed a reason to laugh, for none of us had happy stories about our past that we could tell each other. By then I would have been in the home for less than two weeks and I was still trying to come to terms with the fact that my life was forever changed.

Back in the dormitory, Holly told me more about the Sunday teas – or rather the Sunday teas for the visitors who wanted to have a look at us.

'I saw you looking a bit upset when we were talking about it in the dining room,' she said. 'But it's OK really. And we do get some nice scones and cakes when they come.'

At this, I felt a sharp poke in the ribs.

'So what do they do when they come here?' I asked curiously.

'Sit and talk to us. I suppose they're trying to see if we would be the right one for them to have in their home.'

'Do you really want to go and live in someone's house that you don't know?' I asked, because it was all sounding a bit weird to me.

'I don't think I do,' she said. I realised a bit later why

that was. 'Still, we only go for a weekend to begin with and I know most of the others hope for that invite.'

'Have you been to anyone's house?' I asked.

A question that made her look a bit upset.

'Only once. They seemed all right but they didn't invite me again so I suppose they couldn't have liked me very much. Anyhow I'm happy here.'

Holly was one of the nicest girls I had ever met so I had a problem understanding why anyone would not like her enough to invite back.

'What happens if we don't like the people who invite us to visit them?' I asked.

'Nothing,' she said. 'Matron would never make us go to visit someone we didn't like. Just keep your fingers crossed that you'll meet a couple who will ask you to visit them.'

'But I want to go home when Ma's better,' I said, beginning to feel on the verge of tears. 'Anyhow, I'm going out with Jessica again tomorrow, so I won't be seeing any of them. I suppose Jessica just thinks it's a waste of time for Michael and me.'

She went bright red then and said she was sorry and asked me not to let on about what she had said.

'I'm not a sneak,' I told her. 'Anyhow, I'm coming to church with you first.'

And when I said that Michael and I were going to the farm again, Holly looked wistful – 'Maybe Matron heard that your mother is getting better.'

Holly then started talking about the church and how pretty it was, but it was when she mentioned the priest,

Father John, that I suddenly felt strange. 'Priest' was not a word my mind liked. Nowadays I can understand only too well why that was, but then I couldn't. That night as I lay in bed there were too many thoughts running through my head for me to go to sleep quickly. I was thinking of Ma, wondering when I was going to see her again and at the same time, I tried to work out why the word 'priest' made me feel almost frightened.

When I finally fell asleep, it was more of a drifting experience. One moment my dream took me back home and I was in the kitchen with Ma. She was busy cooking and as she cracked eggs into the flour, I could hear her singing one of my favourite Irish ballads, 'Danny Boy'. Just as I tried to listen, the dream changed and placed me at Maureen's, where I was surrounded by my brothers, before finding myself in a small gloomy room, where all I could see was a pair of dark glittering eyes that made me cry out in fear.

I felt a hand on my shoulder and heard a little voice whispering, 'You're all right, Gerri, you've just been having a bad dream.' For a moment I thought it must be Ma's voice but when I opened my eyes, I found myself looking into Holly's worried face.

As I blinked my dream away, I so wanted Ma to be there then. I wanted to feel her arms around me and hear her soothing voice as she told me I was safe and needed to go back to sleep.

'I get bad dreams too,' Holly whispered. 'We all do.'

She didn't tell me the reasons she had them or why the

others did. Instead, she crawled back into her bed when she thought I had got over that nightmare. Not that I had. For what had begun as a pleasant dream had taken me into somewhere frightening. I could feel my heart racing as I lay there and not wanting to go back into that dream, I was almost too scared to allow myself to fall back asleep. Eventually I suppose I did, but I still felt dazed when I woke in the morning. There was something in the back of my mind that was telling me it wanted me to know something. It took more than five years before I understood that the dream had been made of real memories that wanted to escape from being locked away in the part of my mind that keeps our worst memories hidden from us.

35

Once I was up and had forced my dream to disappear, Jessica came into the dorm saying, 'Come on, girls, time to get ready for church.' Good thing that Maureen had thought to pack my little grey beret and my grey flannel suit that Ma had made for me. She must have been told that I would be going to church regularly.

Jessica left us to clean our teeth and change into our church clothes and then joined us again in what seemed like a few minutes. She certainly looked different from the person I had seen so far, who was always dressed casually in jeans and a sweater, or on warmer days a T-shirt. This time she was wearing a dark blue skirt with a matching top under a cream blazer, her swaying ponytail hidden from sight under a straw boater.

'You look like a model in a magazine,' I told her.

'Thanks, Gerri. You look pretty good too – in fact, all you girls do,' she told us, receiving smiles from all of us.

Once we had finished our breakfast, we left the table to walk to where Matron was waiting for us by the front door. Apart from the navy-blue hat that matched her suit, unlike Jessica, she looked more or less the same as she did every day. With pink scrubbed faces and hair so short it looked more like bristle on top of their heads, the boys who normally had their socks creeping down their legs all looked so neat and tidy as well, I thought.

Matron was right, it was a very pleasant walk. There were fields to the right and left of us, where sheep and cattle grazed, and wildflowers mingled in the hedgerows. I had been told by the others that there was no running or playing allowed on Sundays, we had to walk in pairs and only talk quietly to the one beside us. Once we returned to the home after church we were allowed to read and walk around in the garden, but that was all. I suppose it was because all the children had to look their best when the 'visitors', as the staff called them, arrived at teatime. At least we could take our hats off once we returned to the home, Holly explained.

It was only a fifteen-minute walk to the church, which was in the opposite direction to the way we had travelled before. We turned into a small lane, where we could see the steeple in the distance. Soon, I could see groups of people standing near the entrance, chatting away.

'What do you think of those beautiful stained-glass windows, Gerri?' Matron asked. Looking up to see where light reflected the muted colours, I thought they were wonderful. Matron began telling me a little about the church and just as I was still admiring those windows, I suddenly saw a dark figure dressed in swirling black robes walking towards us. A strange coldness slithered down my spine and I felt my whole body go rigid. I knew Matron and the children behind us were moving forward, but I could not even lift my foot. I felt Matron's hand on my arm and heard her saying, 'Gerri, what's the matter?' But my eyes were glued on that black figure and something stopped anything from coming out of my mouth.

Seeing our group were standing still, the priest began walking towards us. That's when I heard a scream. Had it come from me? I think it must have, just a second before the world went dark and I fell to the ground.

When I came to, I could see a figure sitting opposite me who for a moment I didn't recognise. *Where am I?* was the first question that came into my head. I glanced around to see that I was not outside but lying in a small, dim room that made me shiver.

The moment Matron saw that I was conscious, she moved over to me and took my hand; I held on to hers as tightly as I could.

'Let's get you sitting up,' she said as she helped me up and then put a couple of cushions behind my back. 'How do you feel now, Gerri?' she asked.

'A bit sleepy.'

'Have you ever fainted before?'

'No, what happened?' I asked, completely confused. One moment I had been outside with the other children and I had no idea how I came to be in this room.

'You're in the priest's study,' Matron told me. 'He was really worried about you.' Seeing I still looked puzzled, she told me that I had collapsed outside the church.

'Good thing there was a couple standing nearby. It was the husband who carried you in here. We call what happened "fainting" and you were out cold. And you say this has never happened to you before?'

'No, Matron.'

'Did you have enough breakfast? You didn't have an empty stomach, did you?'

'No, I had eggs and toast,' I whispered.

She paused for a few seconds then said, 'Gerri, was there something in the churchyard that frightened you?'

'I really don't know,' I answered as I tried to remember what had made me faint. 'I think it was those black robes,' I managed to say eventually.

I saw the look of worry deepen on Matron's face when she heard my reply. She didn't tell me I had screamed before I fainted, but Holly told me later that everyone had heard me. Young as she was, Holly was tactful enough not to tell me my scream was one of such abject fear that the whole group went silent with shock. She might not have let me know that, but Michael did. He wanted to know what had frightened me so much that I passed out.

Whatever it was, it was something that Matron wanted to erase from my mind – 'Oh, I've known girls before who didn't like those black robes. They said they had read in the history books that hundreds of years ago, priests had done terrible things during the Spanish Inquisition. Maybe you read about it when you were at school?'

'No, I've never heard of that,' I told her. 'I only know a little Irish history.'

'Well, some children think men in black robes look like a huge crow so maybe that was what came into your head, or perhaps you've had bad dreams about those birds and that's why you seemed so scared. But Father John is a very good man. I've known him a long time and he's very much liked in this parish.'

'I knew the old priest in our village well,' I said. 'He was nice too.'

What Matron must have picked up then was that I had not mentioned the young priest, who had taken over. She must have known then that there had to be a reason I had blanked him from my head.

What I learnt when I turned sixteen and had access to my records was that she made a few phone calls on our return from church. One was to Maureen, who told her that the young priest had been suddenly moved to another parish and that was all she knew. Upon more questioning, she said that yes, Father Pat had often been in our house. And no, Ma didn't really like him, it was my da who was so keen to welcome him in.

I think that was enough for Matron to read between the lines and understand the truth behind my fear and my extensive injuries.

36

There is always a day and what happened in it that remains fixed in our minds. One of mine is that Monday morning when Matron broke the news to Michael and me that not only had our mother died, but we no longer had a family we could go back to. Our father had signed adoption papers for all four of his children. Not that Matron knew that it was our mother who had forced him to do just that, nor did I until much later.

That was the day when Matron finally decided to tell us the truth – although, as I learnt a couple of years later, it was not the entire picture. She told us just enough to help us understand that we were never going back to the place we both saw as our home. I have no doubt that she hated having to see us in her office to break such disturbing news. What I found out later was that it was not only Matron who had decided how much to tell us, it was the doctors and to my surprise, Maureen, who had advised her. They had all agreed at a meeting that it would be best to tell us that Ma had a long illness and had slipped away peacefully in her sleep.

As for Da signing the adoption papers? That was a difficult one, but they came up with the idea that it was because he wanted us to go to a good family – he believed that would be best for all of us. If we asked why hadn't he tried to see us and tell us that himself, she would have to give a good reason. The one decided on was that he would find seeing the children he loved for the last time just too hard to bear.

They all understood that the truth of how and why our mother had died might be revealed to us one day but everyone agreed that we were far too young to know what had happened that night, after I was taken by ambulance to the hospital. Their main concern was me: they agreed that if I learnt the truth, I might well believe that it was me who was responsible for Ma's death and the wreckage of our family.

Matron had been made aware of what had happened to me well before I was brought to the home. The question that had never been answered was just who was responsible for such a shocking crime. Matron had her suspicions, ones she kept to herself. Only a short time before there were three people who knew the answer to that, now there was only two; two who would take their guilty secret with them to their death beds, while I, the only witness, had lost that part of my memory. Yes, I had smelt of alcohol, but the child psychologist at the hospital was convinced that I had buried the details of what had occurred. That also concerned the group, who had my best interests at heart. For what would happen if I remembered everything? They could only hope I wouldn't.

It was Maureen who explained that Matron had considered my loss of memory a blessing. She hoped that the part of my mind which had blocked out what had taken place would remain buried.

I wish it had too.

Matron must have sat in her office wondering how she could tell two scared and lonely children that their beloved mother was dead. There was no gentle way to do it, facts must be told so that we would understand that we would not be seeing Ma ever again. Nor would we be going back to the village where we had been brought up. What comfort could have been given? There was nothing that would have worked. I might not have known then, but I do now, that it's only time that can eventually soften such a brutal blow. Even so, the memory of that day still comes back to haunt me when my eyes are closed and I'm drifting off to sleep. I remember the day so clearly, it could almost have happened yesterday. The moment we were told by Jessica that Matron wanted to see us, I felt sick with nerves. Somehow, I just knew that whatever it was she wanted to tell us, it was not going to be good news.

If I had a hope in my heart of hearts that I was wrong, it died as soon as she gently told Michael and me to sit down. She must have seen how nervous we were for she didn't waste any time in telling us in a very matter-of-fact way that our mother had died.

'You know she was ill for a while,' she said and then without waiting for a reply, she told us in the words that had been decided on that Ma had died peacefully in her sleep. Michael's hands clasped mine and I knew I was shaking, but somehow I was not as shocked as I would have thought I would have been. I think deep down, I already knew; I can't explain why, just that I had felt that Ma had left me all the time I was in hospital.

It was then that Matron began to explain how she and Jessica would do their best to make us feel part of the big family that lived in the home even though she hoped for our sakes that she would find a nice caring couple who would give us a better future. I'm sure that she was aware that we were too shocked to take in everything she was saying. I can remember being too numb with shock and grief to even shed a tear.

Through the fog in my head I could hear her voice saying that Ma had left a letter saying that she wanted Michael and I to stay together. That must have been when I felt a twinge of anger surfacing. What was she talking about? Didn't she know that Michael and I had two brothers? And what about our father? He would be seeing them every day, even if they were staying at Maureen's, so wouldn't he want us back with them?

My nails dug hard into my hand as I asked, 'Why do us two have to stay here anyhow? The doctor said I was better, didn't he? And that's what the nurse in the hospital said, that I had to stay here until I was.'

I felt my brother's fingers grow even tighter around mine

with each word I spoke. It was then that tears begin to prickle behind my eyes as a flashback came into my head: the day Da had not turned up at the hospital and how I had cried and cried. Hadn't he always called me his special girl and given me Flo, my favourite birthday present? So why did it seem he didn't want me back?

I can see my younger self now, sitting on the edge of her seat while her mind refused to accept what she had just heard. She was blinking those tears away as fast as she could because she wanted to hear the answer to her questions. Or should I say she wanted Matron to tell her she had made a mistake and of course she would be going home. She hardly noticed Michael squeezing her hand even tighter as he numbly asked where our family was and why had we been sent to this place when our brothers hadn't.

I can see now that our questions threw Matron off balance. She would have expected tears, but not all those questions. Maybe she hadn't realised that even though our father had been a selfish drunkard, our mother had made our family a loving one. With the closeness in our ages, our brothers and I all played with each other and often curled up together when Ma read us a story. All of us simply adored her and loved listening to her voice. At that time, we both still believed we loved our father, though later it was only Michael who did.

I don't think Matron realised just what a happy family we had been for if she had, would she have told us this next part so quickly? And did she not realise that our lack of tears was because we were suffering from shock and were not ready to hear more? I know that it made me want to scream with disbelief and run out of the room as fast as I could, though I suppose after the questions that had come from me, she felt she had no other choice but to explain why our father had given his permission for all of us to be adopted; that he believed it would be best for us. (Only much later was I to learn that Ma had written another letter telling Da that he had to agree to sign the adoption papers or there was also a letter addressed to the police, telling them exactly what he had done and this would be passed on.)

Before we could catch our breath to protest further, Matron then announced she had good news. At least that's what she called it anyhow when she said in a matter-of-fact way that nice homes had already been found for both our brothers: 'Please try and be pleased for them that they're being cared for by good people. Just a day ago I had news that they're really happy where they are.'

'But when can we see them?' was the next question that shot from my mouth.

'I'm sure that one day they'll get in touch with both of you.'

'But they're only little now, how are they going to do that?'

'When they're a little older,' came the answer. Not that I understood then that unless their adoptive parents agreed, we only had a small chance of ever seeing them again.

'Look, try and be happy for them,' Matron said, which

was hardly a sensible suggestion for there was not a kernel of happiness left inside us. How could she have thought there was when we had just been told that our mother was dead and the rest of our family seemed to have disappeared from our lives?

It was Michael who began to cry. Huge croaking sobs simply tore from his throat as tears poured down his face. I'm sure what he really needed was a pair of arms to go round him. I know I did, but then the arms I wanted were Ma's and what I desperately needed was to hear her voice in my ear; the warm and loving tone that always comforted me when I was distressed.

I don't know what Matron felt when she saw Michael crumble like that. Out of the corner of my eye I saw her pass over a wad of tissues, which he ignored in the depth of his grief.

'I know this is very hard for both of you,' Matron said, before I too collapsed, 'but trust me, Gerri, we're going to look after you here. I see you've already made friends and later, when I feel you're a little more ready, like your brothers we will try and find you a new home with a family who will love and care for both of you.'

'Where is Ma now?' I blurted out then, for I knew enough about funerals to wonder when hers was going to be.

Matron told us that the funeral had already taken place more than a week ago. Another shock for us.

So, she's already buried deep in some hole in the churchyard, I thought dismally.

As if reading my thoughts, Matron said, 'She's resting underneath a beautiful tree, which will always give her shade.'

I should have picked up then that she hadn't told me where Ma was buried but my head was too full of the image of my mother lying all alone in a wooden box. For that's what coffins looked like to me. It was that thought which made the shock take an even deeper hold on me. I couldn't bring myself to say another word, I just wanted to go somewhere Michael and I would be on our own. I couldn't bear the idea that I would never see or hear Ma's voice again.

I could feel his hand still holding mine tightly and I saw that his normally pale face had turned a bright red. Any moment now, if we didn't get away from Matron, he was going to scream out his grief and I wouldn't be able to bear it.

'Come on,' I whispered to him and holding his hand firmly, I made myself stand up.

'The playroom is empty now,' Matron told us. 'I think that would be a nice calm place for you two to sit in. It's too cold today to walk around outside. Jessica will come along to see you a little later.'

Stretching out her hand, she took my free one and squeezed it.

'I'm sorry that you had to hear all this today,' she said, 'but I meant what I said: we will try and help you here.'

I still couldn't find a word to say and holding my brother's hand, his fingers still curled tightly around mine, we walked out of Matron's office. The pair of us managed not to cry as we walked along that wooden corridor. It was me who pushed the door to the playroom open. Matron was right, there was no one in there. Holly told me that evening that Matron had asked the others not to go in there and I must say that everyone was trying to be as kind to us as they could but that morning I felt such a relief that we were alone in that room.

Of all the things that attracted us to sit next to it was a doll's house. Both of us found our hands wriggling inside it and touching the figures. There was a male figure who was the father, a female one wearing an apron and two smaller ones who must be the children. I could see the bedrooms and the kitchen. Tiny it might have been, but it still looked airy. It was when my fingers touched the doll who was dressed as the mother that my tears flowed, as did Michael's. It was the first time I had seen my brother really cry and moving as close to him as I could, I wrapped my arms around his skinny little frame.

We both knew that day that the only remaining relic of our family was the pair of us. At least we knew that we were not going to be separated.

All we had left was each other.

37

Was it that day I wrote the letter to my mother on paper that was spotted with my tears? I suspect it was. It's written on a few crumpled sheets of paper that I have never let go of. Over the years, I take it from the soft cloth bag where it's kept with a few photos. Since I wrote it, I have managed to add a few paragraphs and even corrected the odd childish grammar and spelling mistakes. The change in handwriting indicates not every word was written by an eight-year-old but all the words show the depth of my feelings on that day.

They told me today, Ma, that you are no longer here.

That you left us that night when I was taken to hospital.

I cried and cried but I am writing this now because I feel that whatever they said, you're still with me. I felt you in the ambulance, didn't I? And it was you who was holding my hand and walked beside me when I was wheeled into the operating theatre.

So that's why I know that wherever you are now, you have still not left me.

But, Ma, that will not stop me missing you every single day of my life.

I will no longer feel those gentle cuddles you gave me when I most needed them.

Or those kisses on the top of my head and your arms giving me hugs that helped me fall asleep.

But I know that I will still feel your love, for it will never leave me, will it?

Now my memory is still a little bit jumbled, Ma. There are pictures that float in my head when I'm asleep. There is one from the night when I was taken to hospital. For some reason I was lying on the couch in that room I never liked and I was feeling colder than I would ever have thought possible.

There was a light which must have come from the hall when you opened the door and I saw you walk in.

I can't remember how I got upstairs, I think you must have carried me. I remember feeling you gently washing my body all over and heard you singing, or was it crying? I think you might have done both. I know that when you dried me before you covered me, you lay down beside me and cuddled me like there was no tomorrow before you placed me on my bed and lay down beside me. But then I didn't know that there would be no tomorrow for us ever again, did I?

*You cradled me that night as though I was a baby,
not a little girl of nearly eight. And while we lay there,
you softly sang those soothing songs I always loved.*

*Now when I climb into bed and close my eyes,
it is your face with its gentle expression that I can
see, which makes me know how much I was loved
by you.*

*I can almost feel your hand that was roughened
a little by all the chores you did running its fingers
down the side of my face. I just wish I could hold it
for one more time.*

*When I read this letter again today, Ma, I realise
that I never forgot the final piece of advice you
whispered into my ear that night – never talk about
your parents. Never say anything bad about them,
even if it's true. The world will just turn on you and
put the blame on you. And never criticise a priest,
that would bring you real trouble.*

I thought then that Ma knew something I didn't. But what
was she trying to tell me? Now I know it was a warning,
one she did not want me to forget. But who was it for?

A long time later it dawned on me that it was for me.

And Ma, you were right.

38

When I was with a group of children or sitting with Jessica, I tried as hard as I could not to think about my mother. But try as hard as I might, her smile, her melodic voice when she sang to me and the feeling of her arms hugging me close were hard to banish from my thoughts.

Each morning when I and the others in the dormitory woke, I tried to lock out of my mind the pictures of her and me together. Those were the ones I wanted to examine in minute detail when I was alone. Then I could close my eyes tightly and slowly run them through my mind, which helped me feel her presence.

I yearned for that peaceful time because it let me feel close to Ma.

'I can't tell you just how much I miss you,' I would silently tell her as those treacherous tears of mine fell from my eyes.

I'm still with you, darlin' and I always will be, were the soft words of comfort I heard whispered in my ear.

I might have felt that time alone was important, but

the staff at the home had other opinions. They did not recognise that need in me as being healthy. It was not that they expected or even hoped that I would begin to forget about my mother's death and the family I had lost, more that they were concerned when they noticed me as they thought talking to myself. Maybe they didn't understand that I wanted to be alone so that I could let my mind search my memory box for some of my happy memories. Not just of Ma and me together in the kitchen, or her reading to me in bed, but of my little brothers as well.

I think that Jessica was the only one who understood the reason I needed to be alone but when she saw my tear-stained cheeks, she looked concerned that I might make myself ill. Though surely that was natural? I mean, what exactly would be too much time spent grieving? I know their intentions were good, but all I wished was that they would leave me alone.

It was Holly who was the one who managed not only to get through to me, but also to divert some of my attention from my past to hers. She might have been only a year older than me, but she understood not to ask questions about how I was feeling. Instead, she decided to tell me why she had been brought to the home. That was the best idea anyone in the home had, for it only took a couple of sentences to capture my interest.

I expect one of the staff asked her to chat to me, though I doubt they wanted me hearing something as shocking as Holly's story was. Hearing what she had been through certainly stopped me feeling sorry for myself

– after all, at least my early years had been a great deal happier than hers.

I can remember so clearly how we sat on my bed with our heads close to each other. She certainly didn't want anyone else to realise what it was she was telling me. Her telling me her story began when she accidentally let slip that her parents were still alive. Now that was bound to get a response and it did.

'So, why are you here?' I asked almost snappily for hearing that made me feel almost resentful.

'They were bad to me. So much so, I was taken away from them.'

As I had never heard of anything like that happening, I must have looked rather puzzled. I hadn't worked out that was the reason most of the children in the home had been brought there. But then I was too busy thinking first about my family and then the dreadful news Matron had given us – I suppose I just thought they were all orphans. I hadn't absorbed the snippets of conversation that would have told me quite a lot about the other children in the home. There were all different reasons why they had been taken away from their families – and none of them were good.

Still, Holly succeeded in taking my mind off my pain and getting me curious about her, which was more than anyone else had managed to do. Almost immediately, I wanted to hear just what she meant by the phrase 'bad to me'. Seeing that, she smiled at me before she began her story: 'I was taken away on the same day I was really scared about going home after school. No one warned me about what was going to happen. My teacher knew, but she never said a word about the two women who were going to turn up at our house. I had met one of them that morning and she had been so nice to me when I told her why I didn't want to go home but nothing would have stopped me feeling scared when I heard the knocking on our door.

'Out of the corner of my eye I saw my mother's back stiffen as she quickly glanced out of the window before she moved back from it. If that hadn't told me she knew who was at the door, the curses that flew from her mouth did. With a sinking feeling in my stomach, the question of who was there was spinning in my head. Someone who was very unwelcome, given my mother's reaction, and in my heart of hearts I knew the person at the door had come because of what I had told my teacher.

'With the glare that came in my direction, one of her meaty hands raised up and came down heavily on my head. I knew that it was me my mother blamed, which made me nearly wet myself, I was so scared. She spat out the words, 'What have you been up to, Holly, eh? Been telling stories, have you?'

'I can't tell you just how frightened I was, Gerri. I was trembling all over. I guessed it had to have been someone who I had told things to at school. I tried to tell myself that they had promised not to repeat anything but that didn't stop me being scared.'

'So what had you told them?' I asked curiously.

'I'm getting to that ... Anyhow, before my mother could slap me again, one of the women leant down and called her name through the letter box. I don't know which woman it was, but I heard her saying, "Come on, I know you're in there, Mrs Ferris. We need to talk to you, so would you please open the door?"

'That must have been the first time I had seen my mother, who was such a loud-mouthed bully that none of our neighbours wanted anything to do with her, look unsettled. "Don't you say a word, Holly," she muttered under her breath. She must have hoped they would think they had it wrong and that we were out and then they would disappear. They didn't, though. When there was no response from my mother the letter box rattled once again and we both heard what the voice had to say: "Mrs Ferris, come to the door. It will be better for you if you do. I'm sure you don't want me to call for assistance." In the end, after telling me to stay where I was, my mother opened it. I was even more frightened when I heard her asking just why they had interrupted her when she was busy and what was it they wanted anyhow?

'I wished I could run out of the back door to escape when I recognised Mary's voice asking politely if they could come in. Of course, my mother didn't say yes straight away, her voice simply boomed out so the whole neighbourhood must have heard her shouting, "No, you're not coming in until you tell me what you want," though she did go to the door and stood on the front step blocking them. I saw her shoulders go back when Mary began to tell her where they were from and that they wanted to see me as well as her.

'That was enough to make my mother lose her temper.

She started shouting and cursing at them with her arms flying around, which made it look as though she was going to punch one of them. She's a big woman, my mother – strong too, especially when she's in a rage – and I would have thought those two women would have been scared of her but no, they stood their ground. That's when I saw the man getting out of a car and walking up to them. I heard his voice, not angry, but very firm, telling my mother that was enough. He was holding something in his hand that looked like a sheet of paper. All I know is whatever it was, when he held it up for her to see, she backed off and let the women in. "And I'll be waiting outside," he told her. There was nothing friendly about his voice when he said that. Not that Mary and the other woman stayed long once they came in.'

'Holly, are you saying you left with them?'

'I did.'

I waited for her to tell me some more – I wanted to know who the women were and how come her mother allowed her to walk away with them – but she looked as though she wasn't going to say any more.

'Come on, Holly, tell me why you left with them,' I urged.

'I'm not supposed to talk about it,' she told me.

'I won't tell anyone,' I told her, 'not even my brother.'

'All right then, if you promise not to tell. But the rest isn't nice, you know.'

'So what happened when you came here?' I asked. 'Didn't your ma and da try and get you back?'

'No, Matron explained everything to me. That bit of paper that stopped my mother bellowing was what's called a warrant to remove me from my home. Turns out the man that held it up to her was from the police. I remember I saw her turning her head away – I think she must have seen what I had: that the car the officer had walked out of was not empty. Looking over at what was taking place was another man who hadn't taken his eyes off what was happening on our doorstep.

'Matron told me that when they took me out, my father was already in the police station being questioned. They took him from the workplace because they didn't want him in the house when the social workers arrived; they knew there would have been a frightening scene if he was there. They just wanted to take me out as peacefully as possible. And it wasn't just my dad they had brought in, there was another man they wanted to question as well.'

'Who, Holly?'

'I'll tell you later.'

'Did you know him?'

'Sort of. He came to the house with my dad one night, he was really smarmy and horrid. I told Matron all about him. She didn't look happy but as she had said that I could ask her any questions, I think she must have wished she hadn't because I had plenty of them! Like, why was it Mary who had come to the house and who was the friend she had brought with her?'

'And what did she say?'

'That both of them rescued badly treated children

and some of them were brought here. And before I could ask her, she said, "No, your parents will not be walking through our doors."'

'What happened when they went inside with your mother?' I asked.

'Mary walked right over to me and put her arm round my shoulder. I couldn't help it, I just burst into tears and I couldn't stop. She spoke calmly to my mother and then her friend said that they were going now and I was going with them. And do you know what my mother said?'

I shook my head.

'She came up close to Mary and glared at me and said, "You can fucking well take her! She's the one who's caused all this trouble. Just trying to get attention at school, the fucking little liar!" I thought for a moment that she was going to hit me and so pressed myself closer to Mary, whose arm tightened around my shoulder protectively.

'"Don't worry, Mrs Ferris, she's coming with us," she said coldly. Then her voice changed as she talked softly to me: "You ready, Holly? Anything that you want to bring with you?"

'I said no. She bent down a little then and whispered, "We'll get you new clothes, you can leave everything here," and for the first time since I heard that knock on the door, I smiled. She guided me out of the front door, still holding me close.'

'And you were happy to go with them?' I asked the question even though I could tell she was. I just couldn't imagine what had caused her to be taken away, or what had frightened her so much. None of what I had heard was anything I could imagine. Ma had never been nasty to anyone who knocked on the door and as for my father, I could remember him losing his temper when he was drunk though I preferred to think of when he had given me Flo and taken us all out to the seaside. But I hadn't been frightened like that, had I?

The last thing that Holly told me before we went to our beds was that she was so pleased to get out of the house before her dad came home.

As I have said before, there were several things that caused a cold feeling to slither down my spine. It was as if a deep memory was stirred by some of what Holly had told me and it happened again when she said that she didn't want to be in the house when her father came home. I was uneasy, but why was that? What was buried in my mind? I just knew there was something that I wished wasn't there.

I waited until the next night to ask Holly why she hated going home to find her dad there.

'Because the pair of them would start drinking almost as soon as he came in,' she said.

I was just about to say that Da was a bit of a drinker too before a small part of a forgotten memory of the change alcohol made in him came into my mind. But before I could try to remember a little more, Holly continued: 'Both of them knocked back whatever alcohol was in the house. My mother was never nice to me, but when she was drunk, she was really, really horrid. She was always saying that having me around cost too much. But I don't think it was me who made them hard up, I think it was all the booze they bought.

'I used to put my fingers in my ears when they started shouting at each other. I hated that, because I knew it would probably end up with their fists swinging and if I didn't manage to get out of their way fast enough, a thump could land on some part of me too. Or else they would yell at me to stop watching them and order me off to bed. I'd go willingly even though I often hadn't had any supper. They were always forgetting I needed feeding and if I said I was hungry and asked if I could go to the fridge and get something, I was shouted at. My mother would glare at me and say she wished I had never been born – I think she meant it. She used to moan at having to iron my school clothes or darn a sock. There were lots of times when I turned up at school in grubby clothes and that stopped school being a nice place as well. The washing would pile up, but she was too lazy to do it.'

'Oh, that must have been awful for you,' I said.

'It was because the other kids didn't want to sit next to me, they kept calling me stinky.'

'So is that why those women took you away?'

'No, not really, there was more to it than that. I think it's what I told Miss Davis. She heard what some of the children in my class were saying about me and took me into the staffroom – she must have made sure it was when it was empty. She helped me get my hands and face a little cleaner and at the same time asked a few questions.'

'Like what?'

'Things like what did my mother cook for breakfast today and supper last night. And about what we did at weekends. And she asked if she ever read me stories, that sort of thing. I didn't say anything bad about them. After all, they were my parents and I didn't want to tell her too much but I did a few weeks later. Things had got very bad at home and she must have noticed that I was worried about something. At the end of class she took me off with her again.'

What neither Holly nor I would have understood at that time was that the teachers were told to keep an eye on any pupil who appeared to be troubled or neglected, both warning signals that there might even be something untoward happening in their homes. When she told me about the beatings she had from her mother, I saw tears forming in those bright blue eyes of hers. Hardly surprising, since everything she had said so far about her mother laying into her for no reason sounded so dreadful. I put my arm round her shoulders. Young as we were, at least I had enough sense not to say that Ma would never have done anything like that.

But if I had thought Holly's story was bad up until then, the next part made me shudder. Evidently her parents started locking her in the small cupboard under the stairs.

'What made them do that?' I gasped, for I could hardly believe that anyone would do something so awful to their child.

'They didn't want me around when my father brought a strange man into the house.'

That sentence sent a sudden cold shiver through me. Part of me wanted her to stop right there, but I couldn't bring myself to say that. Holly glanced at me then and continued.

'I knew what was happening. My mother would take the man up the stairs to their bedroom. I'd seen her getting all dressed up and putting on her make-up and loads of perfume. When she saw me looking at her, she took hold of me by the neck and threw me in that cupboard under the stairs.

'"Not one peep out of you or I'll beat that arse of yours raw! Understood?" she'd say each time a man was due to visit. And then she slammed the cupboard door shut and locked it.'

'So, you couldn't see anything?'

'A little, if I pressed my face up to its hinges. But I could hear them. A strange man's voice and then two lots of footsteps going up the stairs. The bedroom door would shut and there would be some noises. I suppose Ma didn't want me seeing or being seen.'

'And how often was that happening, Holly?'

'Oh, at least twice a week. That was when I really dreaded going home when school finished. I hated being in the cupboard, there was no light and I'm scared of the dark. I'm sure there were spiders in there – I could feel something crawling over my hands which almost made me scream, but I didn't dare. That would have got me into even more trouble, so I bit my lip to stop myself.

'But if you think all of that was terrible, it got even worse over the last weekend I spent with them. You know most of us in class keep glancing up at the clock on a Friday because we can hardly wait to be free for two days? Well, that's not how I felt, I just dreaded going home and not going to school over the weekend – there was no escape for me then. My mother made sure I had chores to do so I couldn't wander off while all they did was sit around drinking. I was scared that I would be spending another evening in that cupboard. Instead, on that Friday, I was just told to go to bed.

'It was the next morning when, to my surprise, my mother seemed in quite a good mood. She actually gave me a cooked breakfast and then told me about a visitor who was coming – "Thought you would like to sit with us this evening – you can have a lie-in tomorrow, seeing it's not a school day." Now her being nice didn't stop me feeling nervous. I was used to her mood swings and the slightest thing could make her lose her temper, but not that day. In the afternoon she said she was going to make me look pretty. Not only did she make sure I had a bath, she also helped me wash my hair and for once it was blow-dried – that was something she never bothered doing.

'If I was puzzled by the change in her, I was really amazed when she laid a pretty dress out on my bed – "Saw it in a shop," she told me, "and thought you might like it." And I really did, it was the first nice dress she had ever given me. "You can wear it this evening," she told me with a rare smile. Sounds silly, doesn't it, that I felt a warmth inside me because I was so pleased with that present? All I ever wanted was some attention and kindness, even a few hugs.'

'So what happened that evening, Holly? You said it was worse than all the others.'

'The moment I saw the guest they had told me was coming, I didn't like him and the way he was staring at me just gave me the creeps. He was a big man, thick faded red hair and green eyes that looked me up and down straight away. It sounds silly, but his expression changed when he saw me and he licked his lips.

'"What a pretty wee thing you are," he said, sitting down so close to me that his leg was pressing against mine. "She's certainly a little looker, just like you said," he told my father. Again, I felt those dark green eyes of his running up and down my body and then I felt his sweaty hand patting my thigh and leaving it resting on my knee. Of course, I should have known that the evening was going to be the same as most others. Bottles of drink would be poured and I would either be ignored or snapped at.

'Mind you, I would rather have been ignored than have to put up with that man's hands running all over me and hearing that braying laugh of his. I felt as if he was playing a nasty game with me.

'When my father got up to fetch the second bottle, the man got up as well – "Here, let me give you a hand" was his excuse. As I heard him mutter something about £20 being fair, I wondered what that meant. I pricked up my ears and listened as hard as I could. All my father said was something about school holidays being better than now. He left soon afterwards and I was scared that he would be coming back.'

Holly might not have understood what they meant any more than I did then, but I do know there was something disturbing about her story.

'So how did you manage to come here?'

'It was my teacher, Miss Davis, who told the head that there was something wrong with my life at home. She noticed that I was not concentrating on my lessons and she had spotted bruises on my arms. I must have pushed my sleeves up without thinking because I saw her eyes widen slightly when she saw them. I guess she knew they were fingerprints and that was enough for her to want to find out who had put them there. As soon as the break bell rang, she whisked me off to the staffroom again. She sat me down on a chair opposite her and said she could tell something was troubling me.

'"Is there anything I can do to help?" she asked, but I just shook my head. Then she told me I could trust her and if I said what it was, she might be able to help. Without thinking, I burst into tears. That's when I told her about the man and how I got locked in the cupboard and how scared I was of the men that came round my house. I think I told her everything I could remember. She blinked hard when I told her about the twenty pounds that I heard the man offering my father and him saying about the school holidays. Which were only a week away, she pointed out to me.'

'So what happened after you told the teacher?'

'She told me not to tell anyone what we had talked about and said I wasn't to worry anymore. She promised that she was going to sort everything out for me. She got some tissues out of her bag.

'"No more tears, we'll get this sorted out," she told me. She said she was going to walk me home, which made me quite frightened. What would my parents say?

'"You're not going to say anything to my mother?" I asked her as I thought of the beating I would get if she did.

'"Of course not, Holly. I just want to make sure you come to school in the morning so I'm going to say hello to your mother and tell her that because I'm visiting someone nearby overnight, I'll collect you in the morning so we can walk together to school."

'She did exactly that, was friendly to my mother when she had a few words on the doorstep. Said how well I was doing in school and explained why she would collect me in the morning – "Gives me someone to chat to on the way," she told Ma with a laugh.

'I was not to know then, but that evening would be the last night I would ever spend there. When Miss Davis turned up to walk with me to school, she told me that the headmistress and another woman wanted to talk to me – "They only want to help you, it's nothing for you to fear and remember you've done nothing wrong," she said, giving my hand a squeeze.

'I was worried, Gerri. If Ma found out that I'd been talking about her, there would be real trouble. Miss Davis knelt down so she could look into my eyes and said again, "Nothing's going to happen to you when you go home, you have to trust me. I'm coming back with you again tonight and your mother won't know about anything you've told us." That made me feel a little better even though I had butterflies in my stomach at the thought of seeing the head.

'I was surprised to see her waiting for us in the playground, watching the other children being dropped off by their parents. "I'm going to take you to my office, Holly, so we can chat," she said with a smile and she gently took hold of my hand. Even though she might have been older than my teacher, she appeared just as kind.

'Once we reached her office she sat me down and asked what I had had for breakfast. When I told her a slice of bread with some margarine, she placed a plate of sandwiches on the table in front of me and a glass of milk – "Ham and cheese, hope you like it." I did and she waited for the last crumb to disappear as she sipped a cup of tea. When I sat back in the chair, my stomach felt full for the first time in a long time. The head smiled at me again and explained that Miss Davis had discussed everything with her and there was someone else who wanted to meet me. I felt really nervous then, Gerri. I couldn't think who this person would be and so I asked who it was.

'"Someone who wants to help you. Don't look so worried, Holly, we all want to find a way to help you. That's why your teacher came to me." Just as she said this, there was a knock on the door and as the head called for them to come in, I wished I could make myself disappear.

'I was quickly introduced to a woman who told me to call her Mary as she took a seat on a chair near me. She had curly blonde hair and a round face with dimples and when she smiled, she looked about the same age as my teacher. She told me she was just here to help and chatted to me for a little but I knew she was trying to find out a bit about my home life. There were a few questions that I found quite difficult to answer.'

'Like what, Holly?'

'Well, she saw that I was looking uncomfortable and again told me not to worry and that what was said wouldn't be repeated. I said to her, "They'd kill me if they knew I was talking." I had to try hard not to burst into tears again. I suppose she wanted to be sure that I wasn't making up that story about the man touching me but I could tell almost straight away that she believed every word I said.

'It was when I told her about the money and the school holidays that she asked me what the man looked like. So, I told her about his his faded red hair and green eyes. I said he was older than my father and I knew he played golf because I heard them talking about a golf course near Belfast.

'I saw Mary's eyes blink then – I think now that she knew exactly who he was. She nodded at the head and said her goodbyes. The head said I didn't have to go back to my classroom and I could spend the day in her office doing some drawing and a bit of reading. She kept checking on me and some more food and orange squash arrived at lunchtime. All they told me that day was that things were going to get better for me – I suppose they thought it was better for me not to know what was planned in case I wasn't able to keep quiet.

'Ma was already pissed when the teacher and I arrived. I could smell the gin on her and no doubt Miss Davis could as well. Still, she did her best to sound polite and even offered my teacher a cup of tea.'

'And did she make the tea?'

'No, Miss Davis just thanked her and said no. I saw her glancing at her watch and after just a few minutes, she said it was time for her to go.

'I was pretty scared – Ma must have found it odd that the teacher was back at our house again. I was worried about her quizzing me, but not for long 'cos that's when the two women turned up and one of them was Mary, who I had seen that morning. They took me to a car and brought me here. So now you can see why I was pleased to leave that house and come here ...'

40

I was still of an age when I didn't understand about a child's father bringing in a man to have sex with his wife but there was something about Holly's story that had a familiar edge to it, which was making me feel nervous. It was as though the barrier that blocked my memories to protect me had tilted to one side, allowing just a small flash of unease to surface. Shivers were running up my arms and when I looked down at my arm, it had goosebumps underneath. But I was not ready to talk. We might have been growing up in an age when few children would have understood what Holly was talking about but in a weird sort of way I did. I promised myself again that I would never tell, a promise that I have kept until all these years later when I find myself writing my story.

*   *   *

Another time Holly told me that she had a nice uncle but he left to go to England and no one had his address.

'If he knew where I was, he would come and see me,' she said sadly.

'I know he would, Holly,' I told her more than once.

'My teacher tried to find him for me and so did Mary. I just knew him as Uncle John, I didn't know his surname, but as he and Ma were brother and sister all they had to do was find out Ma's surname before she was married. They did that, but they still haven't found him. That's why I've asked only to be fostered instead of adopted – I think he would take me to live with him if he knew what had happened.'

She told me that she had become scared of visiting strangers' houses (people who might want to adopt her) in case they were the same as her parents and that man – 'The man only has to put his hand on my shoulder and I shudder. I can hardly bring myself to talk to them. I was only asked once and they didn't want me because I was so scared.'

'Are you happy in this home, Holly?' I asked.

'Yes, I want to stay here till I'm old enough to go out into the world.'

That was the end of our conversation that evening. There was so little I could say. The only question that kept running through my head was how come I had known what the man wanted? But I just did.

Don't think about it, I told myself.

41

After Holly told her story, we became inseparable but it was to be many years before she told me how she managed to find the answers to all the loose ends. Although Michael and I spent time together where we shared our memories, it was the closeness I felt to Holly that helped lift the dark despair of my grief. She was the one who woke me up when she heard me having a bad dream and crying out in my sleep and I was the one she trusted never to repeat what she had told me.

I still missed my mother and looked for quiet places where I could be alone and feel her presence but over time, my grief lifted a little and I gradually found that I was able to read a book without my mind turning to memories of her before I had finished one page. I even found myself able to laugh at some of the jokes that came out during those Saturday bath times.

That's good, Gerri, whispered the voice in my head. *Try and enjoy yourself when you can. I want you to be happy.*

That made me shiver a little with pleasure because I felt Ma was still watching over me.

The days the rain clouds disappeared, leaving behind damp grass and small translucent drops of water on the plants in the grounds, I was able to spend time alone with my brother. Whereas other children pulled out the box where their favourite games such as Monopoly were, we ventured outside. Although the other children were friendly and kept inviting us to join in their games, we needed time to be alone or with each other. Like me, Michael felt that what we had to say to each other about our mother and our brothers was private. In fact, it took a long time before we were able to share those memories with other people though years later, I realised that some of them had been completely airbrushed.

Not only were we still grieving Ma's death, we also missed our brothers terribly. I don't think more than an hour went by during our waking hours when they didn't come into our minds. A huge chunk of our life which had been full of friends of our age and people like Maureen, who we had known for as long as we could remember, had been torn away from us.

Michael was not to know that the moment he walked into that hospital to see me, his happy life had come to an end and this was something he eventually became resentful of. When we lived in the home, he never mentioned that. It was not until we left that those thoughts were placed deftly in his mind by another person. But while we lived there, we were more concerned about the unanswered questions that kept creeping to the tips of our tongues when we met with Matron. Questions such as where were our brothers, were they being well looked after, were they happy and weren't they missing us as much as we missed them? Questions that never got a satisfactory answer though we were told they were happy and that the couple who had taken them in really cared for them.

What Matron never told us because she really didn't know any more than what she had already said was that our two younger brothers had been separated and were with different families. I suppose knowing that would have made us feel even worse. We still found it hard to understand why our father had decided that all four of us should be given away to strangers. It was as though we had been a heavy weight on his shoulders, a weight he felt the need to shrug off as fast as he was able. It seemed that for him, forgetting us had not been difficult.

I shared my thoughts with Michael but kept one significant thing from him: I wasn't sure how he would react if he knew how often I felt Ma's presence and how she talked to me. But then he also kept some of his thoughts and wishes to himself as well, though I was not aware of what they were for a long time.

42

As the weeks passed since Matron had told us of our mother's death, I became aware that Michael's depression seemed to have lifted. He told me he was learning to play football at his new school and really liked it. Of course, he had kicked a ball about with his friends for years, but the school had a coach and they played quite serious games now, even though they were still juniors.

He used the phrase, 'It's good fun,' which grated a little. Even when we had been at school in our village, he had never used those words about any of his activities.

During the early weeks in the home, while I was recovering from the operation, I would watch the others setting off on their walk to school. Not that I felt any envy, for I was perfectly content not to be joining them. I was aware that after the time I had been in the hospital I must have been well behind with my schoolwork, which was something I had never been before. That was the main reason that Matron had arranged for me to have lessons on my own with Jessica.

Soon enough I found out that Jessica could certainly manage to do more than one job successfully. Evidently, she had trained as a teacher before she decided she wanted to use her skills to help children recover from their traumas. She must have seen so many bewildered little faces who for various reasons had been taken away from their families. She understood that the distress they had gone through when they were removed had taken away their confidence. And lack of confidence combined with fear of being told off made learning more difficult if not impossible. So, she was the one who tried to get the younger ones ready for school as well as helping the older ones with their homework and showing them ways to aid their concentration.

She also encouraged us all to have more interests by bringing in books she thought we would enjoy reading, taking us for walks so we could learn about flowers and plants as well as letting us watch children's programmes on TV that she thought we would find interesting. Sometimes she would gather us together at the weekend to watch a video. Not one full of happy families but of children who had experienced loss or family problems. Afterwards we would talk about the film and she would explain things more.

Once I began my lessons with her, I felt she was determined that I was going to catch up on my schoolwork so that I wouldn't have the worry of being out of step with the class when I started at the school. After all, I was still only eight, so it was not as though there had been many subjects that I had to learn. Even so, it did take a few weeks before I felt confident enough to join the group and walk with them to school. Or rather, Jessica told me that I was ready to go with the others – 'It will be good for you to be in a proper class,' she said. 'A little competition never hurts.'

On my first day, Jessica walked with us so she could personally introduce me to my teacher, Miss Gallagher, who seemed friendly and welcoming enough. Tall and slim, she had long wavy hair that was tied back in a neat ponytail, and sparkling green eyes. It did take a while for me to feel at ease in the classroom, mainly because during my first years at the village school I had known everyone there. As Holly and the others were in different classes, I had no idea of even the names of the children in mine. I tried hard to remember them but had just about absorbed all the names at the home and now there was a new group of people to learn. But I had done it at the home so I was confident that I could do it again at school.

After a few days of being at my new school I realised what a great job Jessica had done with me. Not only was I not behind but I found the lessons easier than I had when I had been in my first school. I even felt sure raising my hand to answer a question, confident that I had the right answer. That should have made me sleep better, but sleeping was something that I was beginning to be afraid of. I might have been able to control my thoughts during the day, but I had no control over the events that forced themselves into my dreams when I was asleep. I would have been happy if all of them were about when Ma and I were together but that's not what happened. Instead there were dreams that frightened me so much, they forced me to hold my blanket so tightly my knuckles were white when I woke up. Even in my sleep I had tried not to cry out.

There was one dream that came regularly and when I got ready for bed, I prayed it would not come that night. I so dreaded that dream's visits, for not only was there something creepy and intransigent about it, but it was as though it had tentacles that managed to cling to my memory even in my waking hours. And yet it was only a vague outline of a woman standing on the outside of a door; a dark brown wooden door with a shiny brass knob that just had to be gripped for it to open. In my sleep I felt that once my fingers had encircled that sphere, I pushed open the door and walked through it. Try as I might, I was unable to see the woman's face even though my sleeping self struggled to do so. I could feel her grief and despair and then her anger as she pressed her head against the door. In my dream I knew she wanted to kick it open and rush in.

As I lay there, still with my eyes shut and my heart thumping, another shadowy figure appeared. This time I knew it was a man who, ignoring the woman, was running out of that room behind the door.

'Who are you?' I shouted out in my dream.

'You know deep down,' he said over his shoulder and before I could ask again, he disappeared like vapour into the air around him.

That was one of my worst dreams, one that I wished would not return. It made me feel uneasy for more than a day and my concentration at school was non-existent then. I kept trying to identify who he was and why he said I knew him.

There were other dreams that were partly happy and partly sad but even they left a trail of questions behind them, questions that faded away during the day until I couldn't remember what the questions I wanted answered were.

There was one other dream that in my sleep made me feel warm. I was lying on something both soft and firm. It was as if a spell had been cast on me for I couldn't move my hands or legs, nor could I speak. Yet there was no fear in me as under the canopy of my lashes, I could see the figure of a woman walking towards me. I could see her clearly and I knew it was my mother. When she reached me, she leant down. I felt her arms go round me as she pulled me into the warmth of her body and lifted me up where I was lying. My head lay on her shoulder as she carried me, not to the stairs that led to my room but to the door that led outside. Once we were out of the house, she ran as fast as she could without a backward glance at the house that had once been our home. In my dream I knew she was taking me to a place where we could be together forever.

And in the corner of that dream the shadowy man was also there, only this time I saw black robes wrapped around his body as he too ran to the door leading to the outside world. I saw it swing open and as he slithered out, a thousand glittering stars lit up the sky. The dream seemed to have decided to end there but still asleep and wanting to keep Ma with me, I managed to lengthen it. I wanted us to go together to the golden sands close to the flower-strewn Mourne Mountains – the sheep who lived there would welcome us and a mass of white gulls would fly above our heads.

As the dream lengthened, Ma held me so close and then we flew over the star-lit ground until we reached the place that to me was the most beautiful one in the world and she helped me slide out of her arms. I looked around and then wanted to tell her how happy I was. When I glanced back to where my mother had been, she was no longer there. I heard her voice gently telling me that her journey was finished but mine had only just begun. As her voice faded, I knew she had flown away. My dream ended there and feeling the loss of her, I would wake with tears of grief streaming down my cheeks.

There were nights when I hoped the dream would come back and that's what I meant when I said some of my dreams were both happy and sad. It was a dream I hadn't understood as a child, but my adult self has since realised its true meaning. My mother's wish was for me to be taken somewhere safe, where no one could hurt me again. And my wish was for her never to have left me.

43

As much as Matron had promised that she would find a good, caring family for Michael and me to spend the rest of our childhoods with, we remained in the home for just over two years. I can only think that adopting one child is a huge decision and maybe taking both a brother and a sister was beyond most couples.

By the end of that first year, I felt quite settled. I realised that I had no wish to leave there and go to live with strangers. Even though a few of the children we knew had left for their new homes, others arrived looking just as shocked and miserable as we had done. Michael and I now felt part of a big family, with Matron and Jessica fulfilling a need for us emotionally. I enjoyed being at the local school, mainly because with Jessica's help, I was doing well. Then there were the weekends when we went for walks in different parts of the countryside, which I loved and on sunny days, Jessica still arranged picnics at her uncle's farm. All the children were taken there but Holly, who was like an older sister to me, always came with Michael and me. She seemed to have given up her belief that one day her uncle would appear, although I knew there was still a little hope tucked away inside her that he would. But she stopped talking about it.

Holly and I must have been the only two that had little wish to leave the home and we were certainly never short of company or friends. We had our lessons in the day and homework to do in the afternoons. The school was within walking distance so not having to wait for a bus to get us home, we were able to finish our homework and other tasks easily enough before supper time.

I suppose it was being so close to Holly that stopped me trying to develop new friendships at my school. Oh, we were friendly enough when we were in the playground, but it was the invitations to birthday parties I did my best to avoid – I just didn't want to see someone else's home life, I guess, because it made me remember that I too once had one.

When the whole class was invited to a party, I had no choice but to go. Seeing the birthday cake with all its candles being carried out by a proud and beaming mother brought back so many memories of happier times when our whole family was together. I almost burst into tears as I watched the other little girl blow out the nine candles because it brought back vivid memories of my last birthday at home. The one where my father placed Flo, the best present I ever had, in my arms. Standing there, I could almost feel the soft fur on her head rubbing against my hands. I took the first opportunity I could find to say thank you and leave. The mother said she understood I was a little tired and she would phone Jessica to come and fetch me. Those memories of how Ma made our birthdays special flooded my mind and my eyes filled with tears as I waited to be taken back to the home. When Jessica arrived, she did exactly the right thing and gave me a hug before we drove back in silence.

Michael, on the other hand, had started to lap up any invitation he was given. I can picture him as he was then, a skinny frame with sturdy legs striding away from me, shoulders back and a look of determination on his face.

'I'm going, even if you're not,' he would say when the pair of us were invited to one of his friends' homes.

'I don't want to stay in there till I'm a grown-up,' he kept telling me when the Sunday visitors came. 'They won't even talk to us if you don't bother to smile or chat with them.'

I tried, for his sake, but maybe they sensed my reluctance. I think that must have been the beginning of us not being so close and that saddened me.

'If it was just one of us,' he would say more times than I wanted to hear, 'then we might be invited to visit the homes of those who come to see us.'

'You mean we might be taken to live in different houses with different people who don't even know each other?'

'Well, yes.'

'But we don't want to lose each other as well as our brothers, do we?' was my tearful reply.

'Oh, don't be silly, Gerri. We could keep in touch.'

He's taking after his father, darlin',' said the voice.

I know, Ma, and he's even beginning to look like him, I answered in my head.

It was not a nice thought, seeing as Da had signed the papers and with one stroke of a pen, got rid of all four of us.

What upset me most was thinking of all those years when we had never been apart for more than a few hours, the exception being when I was in hospital. And now my brother was making me feel he didn't care if we were separated. From the day he began school and we walked there and back together, I had believed our bond was a tight one but I knew that if I wanted him to stay in my life, I had to face up to the fact that it was loosening. I had to recognise what the problem between us was: he wanted to be adopted and I didn't. Now I understood that I had to wake up to the problem and make a decision because if I refused to act as he wished, Michael might end up being the last one of my family I would lose.

He must have been hoping for some time that one Sunday would fulfil his wishes. That was the one day of the week I had no liking for. I enjoyed the walk to and from the church although a feeling of nervousness still unsettled me when we came within sight of the church. And I didn't enjoy the visiting time in the afternoons. I understood that nearly every other child in the home would be hoping that someone would invite them to spend a weekend in their home – they just wanted to belong to a family. I never told anyone except Holly that it was the last thing I wanted. Some of the children there were so nervous and sensitive that we had to be careful and not let them think we were poking fun at their desperation to belong. So, I went along with them and like all the others made sure I looked my best before I went to sit near Michael in the room where the visitors came. Each Sunday I saw the hopeful expressions on those young faces in the room as the first couple entered. They so desperately hoped that it would be them that they made a beeline for, but it was often a quick smile and a hello as they walked on past to another one who had caught their interest.

To me, it was as if they were window shopping. Did they not think that we all had feelings and dreams of our own? Couldn't they have just looked at photos and asked Matron and Jessica questions about our interests and backgrounds before meeting us? Why did we all have to go through the disappointments when we were not chosen?

Not that many of the middle-aged couples who were interested in older children were good at making small talk to a nervous child about thirty years younger than themselves. And didn't they ever think just how disappointing it was when they talked to one child but ignored another? I felt detached as I observed every Sunday afternoon, and underneath I was quite angry. Imagine the disappointment when a child who had been chatting away to a couple heard they had chosen another. But that was the system back then, a system that worked for a few but made many others even more unhappy.

I can remember hearing children sobbing when they felt it was their fault they had been rejected and on the following Sunday they just wanted to hide away, scared that they would be rejected again. Over the time I spent in the home, Michael and I had only been approached by about twenty people but we were never invited to visit them, doubtless because we were a pair. Michael's disappointment was becoming very evident.

Everyone else wanted to live in a family home, it seemed. I think now that there could have been some bravado there, for apart from me, none of the other ones in there had come from a remotely happy home. That was clear when small, grubby and bewildered children with tear-stained faces first arrived with a social worker. Like Holly, they had been rescued. There was one – Sally, her name was – who couldn't have been more than six. A skinny little red-haired girl who cringed at the slightest noise.

When it came to bath time, we saw the number of bruises which had faded to large yellow ones all over her back and bottom. I could tell Auntie Paula was doing her best to make the child smile a little. She kept chatting to her gently, but I could see flashes of fury on her face each time the child winced – anger at whoever had done it.

Sally eventually told Holly and me that it was her mum's boyfriend who kept hitting her. He also fed his dog some of the food meant for Sally, which explained why she was so thin and hungry when she arrived. We knew better than to ask why her mother didn't stop him. 'No questions' was something that Matron told us each time a new child was on their way to the home.

'My mother wouldn't have done anything either,' Holly said. 'What about yours, Gerri?'

Knowing Holly's past only too well, I felt a bit guilty saying, 'She would have battered Pa with whatever was the nearest if he thumped one of us like that.'

Poor little Sally. Holly and I, like Auntie Paula, tried our best to cheer her up, but how can you make a child who had to be taken from her mother smile?

By then I had come to realise that however awful their lives must have been, most of the children who arrived at the home still seemed to miss their parents and hoped they could go back. They always looked so frightened when they first saw their bed in the dormitory, even more so at bath time. And we heard them cry at night. A happy child might leave the home, but always an unhappy one arrived.

There were times though when a mother accompanied by a social worker would turn up to see their child. It happened in Sally's case and we saw how happy she was when her mum arrived. All three of them went into a private room together. Those visits became regular until the little girl was allowed to leave with her mum. Before she left, Sally explained that the boyfriend and his dog were long gone and her mother had moved to be near her family. So sometimes, but not often, a child's future was worked out.

I still dreaded those Sundays when occasionally someone stopped to talk to Michael and me, but as no one had invited us for a visit, I was quite confident that it wouldn't happen. Not once in just over two years had an invite come our way until that fateful Sunday.

A day that was the beginning of the worst time of my life since my mother had died.

44

It was when we were just finishing our Sunday breakfast that Matron came up to the table where Holly and I were sitting.

'After your breakfast, Holly, come to my office. I have some news for you,' she said with a wide smile that told us it was good news.

'What is it?'

'You'll have to wait till you've finished your breakfast, dear,' she told her and off she went, still with a smile on her lips.

I saw the excited look on Holly's face and knew as she did that there was only one bit of news she wanted to hear. I never saw her gulp her food down so fast.

With that, she got up from the table and rushed out, leaving me with a bit of a sinking feeling as I too had guessed the reason Matron had asked her to come to her office. I had an even bigger clue when she bounced into the dorm where we were all getting ready for the walk to church.

With her face flushed and her eyes sparkling, I knew what Holly had been told and I could see that she couldn't wait to tell me.

'You'll never guess what's happened, Gerri,' she said as she flung her arms around me and gave me the widest smile.

Of course, I wanted to believe it was something different, but I knew it wasn't.

'Matron had a phone call from Uncle John – you know, the one Miss Davis was trying to find all that time ago. And he's coming today! He's going to take me out for tea. He told Matron he's got a lot to tell me.'

'Did he find you, or was it Miss Davis who found him?'

'No, Gerri, my uncle found me. Matron told me how it happened and she was laughing! Can you believe, she was just so pleased for me.'

Something told me that Holly's uncle coming to the home would end up being more than just a visit. From what she had told me, it was more likely he would want to take her away.

Be pleased for her, whispered the voice.

I'll try, Ma, I answered.

Which I did. I put a smile on my face and hugged her back.

'That's wonderful, Holly! You must be over the moon,' I said.

'I am, Gerri. I can hardly believe it.'

'Did Matron tell you how he found you?'

'When Miss Davis tried to find him, I hadn't known

that he and my mother had different fathers. My grand-mother's first husband, who died in 1939 in the war, was John's father. Then she remarried and became a Ferguson and my mother was born, which meant they had different surnames. I should have guessed really, seeing they're not a bit alike. He can't stand her, I knew that. Not that he ever said so, but I sensed it all right and I think he only came round her house to see me. He's really kind. Anyhow, that's the reason – I gave Miss Davis the wrong surname. He was working up in the north of England and as he had a few days off, he decided to get on the ferry and come to see some of his old friends and see me too.'

'What does he do?'

'He's a builder.'

'So, do you know now what happened? Your mother would hardly have been helpful, would she?'

'Yes, sounds like he did have a bit of a job finding out where I was living. Matron told me it hadn't been that easy, but he was determined to find me. He'd gone round to where my mother lived. Well, she practically slammed the door in his face. That was my mother for you. Of course, he had no idea that I was no longer living with her so he went up to the school, thinking he could meet me there. Instead, he found Miss Davis and she told him I'd been taken away. She might not have told him everything, but he would have known that my parents must have treated me very badly for social services to be involved – I think he must have been very angry when he heard. Anyway, he got in touch with Matron on Friday. She wanted to talk it through with social services and also make another call to him confirming his visit before she told me about it just in case he changed his mind. But he didn't and now I can't wait to see him.'

I knew from all the gabbling and the expression on her face that she was certain he would be taking her away with him.

On the way back from church I had to pretend that I was happy for my friend. Well, in a way I was, it was just that we had become so close since she told me her story and I knew just how much I was going to miss her. Holly must have felt that too, for she linked her arm in mine and smiled at me.

'You'll have to meet him,' she told me. 'I know you'll like him.'

Like him or not, I couldn't help but wish him away, though I did manage to tell myself I was being selfish and mean and that I should be brave and think about my friend's happiness.

As we finished our walk and arrived back at the home, Holly nudged me. 'Look, over there,' she said. And following her gaze I saw a tall dark-haired man standing near the doorway. I could feel Holly's breath on my cheek as she opened her mouth to shout out his name and I thought she was going to take off and run up to him. Something must have stopped her though and instead of running, she walked with the rest of us up to the door before breaking ranks and dashing to her uncle.

His arms shot out and wrapped around her as he gave

her a hug, lifting her feet off the ground. I saw how her head was pressed against him, for wasn't he the only person she had so wanted to see over the last few years? Finally, she would be cared for by someone she really loved and who loved her in return.

45

Later, when we were getting ready for bed, Holly said that the moment she saw her uncle waiting for us, she wanted to run to him as fast as she could but she thought it might upset some of the other children who didn't have any nice relatives who came to see them.

'Not that you have either,' she said, giving my arm a squeeze, 'but at least you have a brother and you have me.'

I managed a smile through my sadness at what was to come. But my friend was so kind and thoughtful, even when something so good was happening to her. Then she told me of her plans and how she and her uncle had discussed how we could do more than just stay in touch by post. I knew she was worried about what she had to say, knowing it would be upsetting for me.

And I was right: he was going to take her to England with him. He was married and had been for a couple of years; his wife was looking forward to meeting her.

'She's sent me a message saying she's looking forward to me coming to their home and she's getting a room ready for me. And here's a good bit of news: my uncle says you'll be welcome to come and visit during the school holidays. He has spoken to Matron and she can make it happen. He'll organise a ticket for you and he and I will drive to pick you up from the ferry.'

That made me feel a little better.

'And he wants to meet you before I go, so he's coming over tomorrow afternoon to pick us up from school and taking us out for tea. The same place he took me, where there's loads of scones and cakes and the best ice cream I've ever had. Really scrummy, Gerri! You'll will love it, and you'll love Uncle too.'

I must admit that I still had a little resentment of him being there, but I couldn't help liking Holly's uncle straight away. I could see how fond he was of his niece and I could also see that it was obvious that they were related. Like her, he had thick black hair and dark blue eyes, fringed with thick lashes.

I wondered how much she had told him about me for, like her, he spoke firmly about the invitation to visit Holly in his home. And I just knew by the expression on his face that he was a kind man who meant every word he said. We chattered away and he told me that he realised I was very important to Holly and he would be looking forward to seeing me in the future, which made me feel that even though I would miss seeing her every day, some of my feelings of impending loss had been lessened. He explained that he would not be there for long, but he had to stay for a few days extra as he had an appointment with social services.

As I found out several years later, he needed to bribe Holly's mother to agree to her living with him and to make it clear to social services that was what she wanted. Goodness knows how much he paid her, but it worked out and Holly was gone less than a week later.

* * *

On the day that she left, Holly and I were both in tears and hugged each other tightly, making promises of frequent letters. Long after they drove off, I sat on my bed with tears streaming down my face. I kept telling myself that I still had a visit to look forward to and we would be writing to each other, wouldn't we? But no matter how many times I said it to myself, I still knew nothing would be the same without her.

Just about the last words Holly said to me were that she would write as soon as she had unpacked. True to her word, a letter came. She told me how lovely her room was and how nice her uncle's wife was and how she knew she would be happy there. '*But I miss you, Gerri,*' she wrote, which of course brought more tears to my eyes, for I already missed her badly. But that didn't stop me getting out my notebook and writing her a letter in return, which I tried to make as cheerful as possible. Little did I know that would be the only one she would ever receive from me. Not that I was to find out for a long time.

46

What changed my life again was when, on the following visiting day, I met a couple called the Donaldsons. And no, it wasn't a good change – far from it, in fact.

It was a week after Holly had told me about her uncle and five days since she had left, when on a dark cloudy Sunday afternoon, Michael and I met them. To this day, I wish it had never happened.

I suppose if Holly had not gone all the way to England with her uncle, I might not have responded so easily to the Donaldsons' invitation to visit them, but I was at a very low ebb – I missed Holly more than I thought was possible.

I don't like them, Ma, I said silently when they came over to where Michael and I were sitting.

Nor do I, whispered the voice in my ear.

If only I had told Matron what I really felt. Which I might have plucked up the courage to do had the Donaldsons not chosen that time to approach us. Missing Holly as I did made me more vulnerable and I knew Michael wanted to accept any invitation to a visitor's home; I needed his company so much then and he would get angry with me if I refused to go.

Somewhere deep down I felt it was not me they wanted in their house, it was Michael. I had seen the warmth in Mrs Donaldson's eyes when she spoke to him, which was missing when she turned to me. Still, they must have known when they introduced themselves about the papers our father had signed, stating we had to go together. We both knew that one of the reasons we were still in the home was because any couple who came hoping to find a suitable child would be told that we must stay together. My brother had certainly let me know more than once that it annoyed him that I was apparently the obstacle to him being adopted.

On those afternoons I usually had a book on my knee – I suppose I must have been trying to appear as disinterested in those visitors as possible. Michael on the other hand was pretty good at giving wide, hopeful smiles to them. It certainly caught the attention of the couple I had noticed coming into the room and I realised that they kept looking over at us.

Don't smile at them, I felt like saying to Michael. Too late, they were already making their way over. To me, they did not look in the least bit interesting; they were about the same age as our parents had been the last time I saw them, but that was about the only thing they had in common. With her mousy hair worn in a short bob, the woman looked nothing like Ma, who liked to wear pretty, bright-coloured clothes whereas this one was dressed in a frumpy grey suit. I guessed she and her husband were churchgoers as he, a slight man with dull brown receding hair, was wearing a black suit. Certainly, they didn't look like fun people to me. As they walked towards us, I saw them ask Jessica something and her smiling and answering them, as all three of them turned to look at us.

I tried my best to keep my head down so I appeared to be engrossed in my book, but that didn't stop Michael from nudging me in the ribs as he cast his gaze in their direction and whispered, 'I think we have visitors.'

It was the woman who smiled and spoke first: 'So, you two are brother and sister? The young lady over there told me that you're a very close pair.'

'We are, I suppose,' my brother piped up with his broadest smile, which told me he wanted them to take a liking to both of us.

'Well, let us introduce ourselves: we are Mr and Mrs Donaldson. And you two are …?'

'I'm Gerri,' I answered, forcing my lips to curl into a smile.

'And I'm Michael,' my brother chipped in enthusiastically.

'Mind if we join you?'

'Of course not,' we both said. Not that I was being sincere, but being polite to visitors was a rule that no one dared break. And I could tell that my brother so desperately wanted them to talk to us that I had to play along with it.

'I can see you've been reading,' Mrs Donaldson said to me as I politely put my book to one side and looked up at her face, where a pair of thick-framed glasses were perched on a bony nose. Her smile was friendly or perhaps it was trying its best to be. 'Enid Blyton, I see.'

'Yes, this one's all about the Famous Five – our library has quite a few of her books,' I replied with some enthusiasm.

They seemed to want to know what our interests were. Not that the husband had much to say, he left most of the talking to his wife, but at least he smiled at us several times and asked if we liked country walks. That was an easy question. I found myself telling them how much I had enjoyed the farm Jessica took us to – 'I love being around animals,' I told them – and then for some reason I couldn't stop myself from telling Mrs Donaldson about the day I had been given a kitten for my birthday: 'Flo, she was called, and I loved her.'

'Oh, we were thinking of getting a dog,' Mrs Donaldson told us. 'One would make us go out walking more, wouldn't it?' she said, turning to her husband.

'Eh, yes, of course,' he answered and I had a feeling this was the first time she had mentioned it to him.

Of course, Michael butted in, saying how much he liked dogs too. We both said we enjoyed having picnics in the countryside and Michael told them he loved going to the sea but he didn't like busy beaches because he wanted to be able to walk and feel the sand beneath his toes. I thought he must be remembering one of our days out near the Mourne Mountains and the memory immediately made me feel sad.

The Donaldsons mentioned a few places they liked and managed to keep the conversation going for the rest of the visiting time when we moved to a table to have our afternoon tea. Michael and I couldn't resist tucking into fresh scones with dollops of jam while I noticed the Donaldsons hardly ate anything, just sipped away at their tea while we drank orange juice.

They patted our shoulders when they got up to leave and told us they had enjoyed our company. When they walked out, they were the last of the guests to go. Michael looked really excited after their visit: 'I think they liked both of us,' he kept saying. 'Do you think we might hear from them soon, Gerri?'

'Maybe,' I muttered.

I really hoped we wouldn't. They might have tried to be as nice as possible, but I hadn't felt one ounce of warmth coming in my direction. Unfortunately for me it only took them twenty-four hours to contact Matron. She called us both into her office to tell us that we had been invited to spend the weekend with them and that they wanted to collect us on the Friday evening.

Michael looked as though he was about to jump up and down with joy when he heard that, while for me it was just the opposite. I hadn't taken to them at all nor had I felt, despite them talking to both of us, that they wanted me.

You could tell Matron you're not happy going.

I can't upset Michael like that, Ma, look how excited he is.

So, I tried to appear pleased.

It was Jessica who helped me choose what to pack in my case. Evidently a new dress had arrived for me.

'Who sent it?' I asked.

'Oh, just someone who donates clothes to us,' Jessica told me.

I found out when I turned sixteen that Jessica had bought it from the money that Maureen had sent to Matron to buy new clothes when I needed them. And Matron had rung and told her about the Donaldsons. But then I had no way of knowing that she and Matron had kept in touch so that Maureen could be kept up to date with our progress.

Well, fingers crossed I can put up with them for two days, I said to myself as we waited downstairs.

There were smiles from Mrs Donaldson when they arrived, while her husband placed our luggage into the boot. I suppose they must have been in their early forties, but to me, they looked quite old and they also seemed rather strange. In all the time I was to know them, they never talked about their families and they had no children of their own.

It was quite a long drive to their home, a large modern redbrick house set back from the road with the neatest garden I had ever seen. Not that I was too surprised by that, any more than I was when we went inside. Huge landscape paintings hung on the white walls of a tiled large hall. Impressive, but cold, I thought, for there was nothing homely about their house. I couldn't imagine them having a dog in it either – muddy paws and dog hair would not suit this pristine place. As they showed us around, Michael seemed to think it all looked wonderful though – 'I can't believe I'm in such a great house!' he exclaimed.

First, we were taken into the big kitchen with its dark slate flooring and immaculate white cupboards, then into the sitting room with French windows and a brick fireplace that seemed huge to us. Needless to say, there was nothing out of place anywhere. Mrs Donaldson then took us up to show us our bedrooms, each with its own bathroom. Michael just about gulped when he saw that – it was a place like no other we had ever been into. We had seen a few houses bigger than ours when we went to parties, but nothing on this scale.

'Come on down when you've unpacked,' she told us.

There was certainly plenty of room in our empty wardrobes to hang up our one change of clothes.

In my room there was a single bed with a pale pink duvet. Like the downstairs, the walls were white and there were no ornaments or pictures. It felt large and empty and to me a little strange not to hear the chatter of the other girls in it. It was then that I saw a small square table with a lamp and a book on it by my bed. When I picked the book up, I saw to my delight that it was the latest Enid Blyton, which I had said that I hadn't read yet. Our library books were donated so we rarely got new books in the home. I have to say that pleased me. *Maybe she's nicer than I realised*, I thought hopefully. Still holding the book, I went downstairs to thank her.

'I'm pleased you like it, Gerri. I remembered you told me you liked her books and it's good to see children reading – I did that a lot when I was your age. I still have some, I'll show you.' Then she took me to a smaller room, which had a desk and bookcases inside. Bending down, she pulled out a book and I could tell by its cover it was a very old one. 'It's a first edition,' she told me, opening the book carefully to a page that said 'First edition published in 1868'. 'It was the very first of a series about a group of children. You can see it's called *Little Women*. It was my mother's and she gave it to me when I was about your age. I'm sure Enid Blyton read them when she was a child too. So, when you visit again, you can read it when you're here.'

And that was the beginning of Mrs Donaldson making me feel welcome. Or should I say that it was a very good act, one that almost succeeded in making me trust her.

Don't, whispered the voice.

So, I didn't.

The Donaldsons certainly worked hard at impressing us that weekend. 'Got a surprise for you two, we're taking you to a film,' Mr Donaldson announced. Michael was thrilled when told we were going to see *The Jungle Book*. But it was not just him who enjoyed that film, I simply loved the music in it.

On the Saturday they took us out to an old cottage serving afternoon teas.

'I saw how you liked scones and jam,' Mrs Donaldson told us.

On the Sunday morning, they drove us back after breakfast.

Had we had a good time?

I suppose so.

Had I begun to like them?

No.

Even though the Donaldsons had acted as friendly as they could, it was only Michael who wanted to be with them.

Why did I feel that? I don't know. And why did I not tell Matron that I would rather stay in the home? That was the biggest mistake I ever made.

We had one more visit and then we moved in.

47

It took less than a week for me to regret moving in with the Donaldsons. We had been collected from the home late on the Friday afternoon and were shown into the same rooms we had slept in before. This time we had a little more unpacking to do and at least, unlike the home, there were plenty of drawers and wardrobe space for us to put everything tidily away.

I placed the doll that Maureen had brought into the hospital for me on top of the chest of drawers. She had once been so precious to Ma and now was even more so to me. I chose that spot because it meant that when I lay in bed, I could take comfort in looking at her just before I went to sleep; I almost felt that saying goodnight to her was like wishing Ma goodnight. After making myself look as neat as possible, I went downstairs with Michael following behind me – 'Don't you love having your own room?' he whispered. 'I can't believe it's so big!'

'Yes, it's great,' I lied. To me, it was a big and empty space and already I missed the girls in my dorm.

Smiles came in our direction when we walked into the kitchen, where Mrs Donaldson was chopping vegetables. 'Just getting supper sorted out,' she told us. 'You can both go in the lounge and relax for a little while I get this finished.'

Luckily, I was clutching a book in my hand, for any hope of watching TV went straight out of the window when we saw it wasn't switched on. Neither of us had the confidence to ask, let alone do it ourselves. Although Michael eventually managed to master switching it on, I never felt I could.

So, what was our first day of living there permanently actually like? It seemed all right, I suppose, but was there something in the atmosphere or was it the way Mrs Donaldson glanced in my direction that made me feel uncomfortable? The answer, I believe, was both, although I couldn't grasp that then. I was aware within minutes that the Donaldsons' conversation, unlike Ma's or Maureen's, held little humour. And as for watching TV, it appeared the only programme they were interested in was the news, which meant long discussions between the two of them about what had taken place in the world, although their main interest was Irish politics. There were lots of remarks about the trouble that the Catholics were creating, which made me squirm.

'Oh, sorry, Michael,' Mrs Donaldson said, 'I forgot your parents were Catholics, but I'm sure they were different from the ones we were talking about.'

'Oh, that's all right, Mrs Donaldson. Not something my

ma or da talked about,' he told her. 'They didn't like what was happening either.'

And that was the beginning of them not including me in their conversations. By the time the weekend was over, I realised they did not speak to me directly any more than they could help. Despite this, I did my best to be as good as possible – like when the meal was finished, I offered to help clear the table and wash up.

'That's all right, Gerri, I can manage. As you've brought your book down, you might as well sit and read it until bedtime,' Mrs Donaldson told me.

On the Saturday morning Mrs Donaldson told us we were all going out for a walk. Michael immediately piped up that it sounded great and I managed to sound as though I agreed with him, even though I was wondering what kind of a walk they had in mind. The moment we set off, I could see it was not going to be the same as the wonderful walks we did with Jessica. Without the chatter that I was used to, I found it boring. Their intent was to have a bracing walk, while I liked to look at the animals in the fields and the flowers at the side of the road. Michael seemed to enjoy being with the couple and strode off at their pace with me trailing behind.

I know you're bored, said the voice, *but try and make the best of it, darlin'*.

I will, Ma.

I think I already had some idea of what type of woman Emily Donaldson was, even before Sunday arrived. There was no mistaking she was one of those tight-lipped, small-minded church-goers who look down their noses at those who do not turn up to church every Sunday. The one conversation she had with us that made my ears prick up a little was about her religion. Hadn't Matron told us that their religion was different to ours? I think she mentioned they were Methodists and Michael and I had said we didn't care. But maybe we should have asked a little more, for the Donaldsons made it clear that consuming alcohol was a sin, as was watching anything except the news on TV or listening to any modern music on the Sabbath.

By the end of this conversation, I knew that Mrs Donaldson's views were strict ones, but on the way to church, I also found out that she was the sort of woman my mother had little time for. I could remember Ma saying quite crossly about one of the women in our village that she never had a good word to say about anyone and that she really didn't want to listen to her.

And that Mrs Donaldson's just like that. Told you I didn't like her, came the voice.

Nor do I, Ma.

With a ramrod straight back, Mrs Donaldson walked with us to the church, dressed in the kind of drab dark outfit I thought more suitable for a funeral than a Sunday service. I could hear her muttering away to her husband as we passed those who were spending the day at home. 'Just look at them doing their gardening and cleaning their flashy cars on the Sabbath. Disgraceful!' she kept saying with a disapproving sniff, which for some reason irritated me no end. Not that her remarks seemed to bother

Michael, quite the opposite. I could hardly believe it when he kept nodding his head in agreement. For a church-goer, she seemed quite intolerant and bad-tempered.

When the service was finished, we left without lingering. I wondered if that was because no one there except the minister had tried to engage the Donaldsons in conversation when we walked outside. Small groups of people were chattering away, but we were not called over to join any of them.

The minister was a tall man, whose dark-blond hair was cut so neatly, I wondered if he trimmed it himself every day. It seems so strange to me that apart from his white collar and black top, he was dressed in normal clothes. The church and the service were also so different to the ones we had attended before. He uttered his thanks to the Donaldsons for being there – 'Such devout Christians you both are,' he told them with a warm smile – and I noticed that neither of them told him who we were. But they had their reasons, which I was unaware of then.

As we walked back to the house, I could hear Mrs Donaldson resuming her muttering and it seemed that she became louder as she uttered unpleasant remarks accompanied by a disapproving sniff about just about everyone we met. She even complained sourly about small children squealing with laughter as they played together in their garden – 'Don't you think they're old enough to have gone to church with their parents?' I heard her ask her husband. 'If their parents can't be bothered bringing them up as good Christians, I doubt they will grow up to be good people.'

And what do you think she asked me then? I was so taken aback, I couldn't think of an answer to give her.

'Oh, I suppose you don't care,' was the beginning of the many snubs that seemed to come only my way. Not that I understood then why that was, I just let Michael walk beside her while I strolled along behind them. Nor did it stop me from hearing another one of her insults when she saw a couple of boys about my age cycling up and down a peaceful side street. 'Just what kind of families do they come from?' I heard her saying loudly to both Michael and Mr Donaldson. Seeing the boys had heard her, I cringed with embarrassment – I just hoped neither of them would be at the same school I was due to attend.

She must have had her ears well and truly cocked for if she heard one beat of pop music coming through the windows of a house, her disapproving sniff became even louder. 'Scummy' she called that type of music and later on if she ever caught Michael and I watching a programme like *Top of the Pops*, she voiced her disapproval again and turned off the TV.

I remember one evening when he and I were just about glued to the TV when Rod Stewart appeared on a chat show and was asked to perform. Wriggling away as the music started, he let rip with his gravelly and mesmerising voice. That was enough to make Mrs Donaldson rush into the lounge and turn it off.

I can still hear her voice ringing in my ears saying, 'I don't want either of you listening to a singer like that.' And then my brother, with his new smug smile piped up, 'Oh, I don't want to watch him either.'

I just stared at the blank screen wishing the programme was still on, which caused me to receive a look of contempt. It seemed Michael was certainly doing his best to please this woman who had none of the same interests that we had and not an ounce of humour. I knew he really wanted a home, but why did it have to be this one?

48

It took me just a short time to realise that the only reason I was in the Donaldsons' house was because Emily Donaldson had taken to Michael straight away. I'm sure she would have liked to have taken him alone, but she had no choice other than to agree to have me too as we came as a pair. The only time she appeared to show she was happy with her choice was when their house had been approved and the four of us were meeting with Matron. I could feel that bony hand of hers resting lightly on my shoulder as she smiled down at me. That was enough to give the impression that she was delighted I was going to be part of their family. Talk about a good act! I suppose then she wanted all of us to believe it, but even so, she didn't fool me. I believe her fondness for my brother was genuine though. The truth was I didn't really like her, even though up until then she had been as pleasant as she could. *Still, I will have to make the best of it*, I kept telling myself. *After all, it's a lovely house.*

I felt a little nervous at the thought of having to start at a new school again, where I wouldn't know anyone. How I wished I could talk to Holly about it, but as I couldn't, I sat on my bed and wrote her a long letter in which I tried my best to make it sound as though I had moved into a house where I was happy. Once I had written it, I went to Mrs Donaldson and asked if she had an envelope I could use to send a letter to my friend – back then, I had no money (we were only given bus fares and dinner money to give to the school).

'Dear, just give it to me, I have to go out shopping today so I will post it for you,' I was told.

'How long does it take to get to England?'

'Oh, just a couple of days.'

'And does it take the same time for one to come here?'

'Yes, about the same.'

I calculated that a letter from Holly would arrive on the fifth day. Every time I heard the letter box snap shut, I would rush to the door, where Mrs Donaldson was already picking up the mail, and be told there was nothing there for me. Nor was there anything the next day or the day after that.

Surely, Holly's not forgotten about me already? I asked myself.

Although I was beginning to feel tearful, I wrote her another letter. I tried to sound cheerful, saying how much I missed her and how I was looking forward to seeing her when the summer holidays came and I would go to visit her in England. This was something I had not got around to telling Mrs Donaldson although I did think then that she might be pleased if I was away for several weeks because she would have Michael all to herself.

Maybe it was shyness that stopped me telling her or perhaps it was the fact that I still hadn't received a letter. I waited and waited every day for the post to come with a letter for me. None arrived and I sank into a bit of a depression.

A depression that began to increase when I felt that my presence in the house was only tolerated and by no means liked. Something it didn't take long for me to realise. There was nothing nasty said to me, just niggling remarks that got under my skin. Like thinking Mrs Donaldson would be pleased when I asked if I could read one of the children's books she had shown me.

'Yes, but remember they were my mother's and I don't want them damaged,' she warned in the tone of voice that suggested she didn't trust me. And yet I remembered her telling me I could read all of them whenever I wanted to.

Then there were small reproofs such as after I had brushed my hair and dressed it to the side like Ma always did for me. Mrs Donaldson told me to tie it back – 'Makes you look scruffy,' she said, which embarrassed me. And when I asked her about the new school, she snapped, 'It's the same as any other! After all, you've been to more than one, haven't you?' Again, her tone of voice made it sound as though it was in some way my fault that we were going to a new school.

And when I put on the dress that was my favourite colour of blue that Maureen, unbeknown to me, had sent, she looked me up and down critically: 'That colour doesn't suit you and it's also a bit too tight.'

There's a way, isn't there, of taking away another person's confidence in small but frequent stages? She was certainly an expert in that area and understandably it didn't take long for me to feel nervous around her.

'The school you and Michael are going to have agreed that you can wear the uniform you already have,' she told me one day.

I found this disappointing, for after wearing my grey school skirt for quite a while, I had to have the hem let down twice, which made it look rather shabby. Of course I would have liked to start my new school looking smart and fitting in with the other pupils, but knowing this would just annoy her, I kept quiet.

The last remnants of pride I still clung to would not allow Mrs Donaldson to see just how upset I was when she took Michael out shopping to buy a brand-new school uniform. She even picked out an expensive-looking satchel for him too. While my hair grew longer and more difficult to control, they returned from this outing with Michael sporting a very stylish haircut.

'Don't you think his hair cut makes him look smart, Gerri?'

I nodded bleakly.

49

Relief came a few days before the social worker was due to check up on Michael and me. All those barbed comments ceased to come out of Emily Donaldson's mouth. She was too careful to continue her strategy of breaking my morale for she wanted the social worker to see a nice, happy little family, which we wouldn't be if one of us was downcast and tearful. We were never left on our own with them – Mrs Donaldson was always in and out with cups of tea and the social workers all thought the house was lovely.

Anyway, on the days when she knew that a social worker was due, Emily Donaldson would ask us what we would like to eat for breakfast and then it was 'Sit down, both of you' and she was all smiles as she plonked down glasses of orange juice and a bowl of fruit salad. Not long after a large cooked breakfast was placed in front of us, the doorbell would ring and I would hear her chirping away as she welcomed in the social worker.

So, she actually has the ability to turn on some charm, I thought.

Charm that stayed with her when she put her head round the door and told us to join them both in the lounge once we had finished our breakfast. Her voice was warm and friendly throughout the visit. When the social worker asked each of us if we were happy in our new home, not wanting to rock the boat I put on a fake smile and said that I was. Michael, on the other hand, was totally sincere when he told her that he really loved being there – little wonder with all the special attention he got.

Always the memory of how Michael had snapped at me in the home when he thought I might stop us living with the Donaldsons stuck in my mind and it was that which prevented me even giving a hint that I wanted out of that place – I just couldn't bear the thought of losing him. Maybe if Holly hadn't appeared to have vanished from my life, I would have had more courage. I not only missed her, but Jessica as well – in fact, I missed just about everyone in the home.

During those first few months, the social worker visited regularly and I refused to accept that my brother was slowly distancing himself from me. But then I didn't believe that the small boy I once walked to school with, the one who had a torrent of tears running down his face when he was told about Ma, and the one who stayed glued by my side afterwards, was no longer there. Another boy had taken his place, one whose dormant craftiness had been awakened – and that boy was the opposite to the one I had loved so much.

On these visits Michael went out of his way to make

sure he made me laugh a little and chattered away to me. 'Do you remember, Gerri …?' was one of the lines he came out with when he brought up a little story of our earlier days when something amusing had happened. More than once he mentioned Ma's singing in the kitchen and I like to think that part of him was genuine. He even grabbed hold of my hand a few times when we were talking. Him being like that made me feel much more cheerful so that when the social worker sat with us, I managed to be all smiles.

The only reason I didn't ask to be sent back to the home was because I believed not only did Michael still need me, but that I would miss our closeness too much if I left. I realised my mistake within a matter of days when that closeness I had so believed in evaporated into thin air within days of the social worker's final visit.

When did I see the change in him? About a couple of weeks after Emily Donaldson told us that she doubted there would be any more visits from social services – 'They have more important work to do,' she explained, 'rescuing innocent children from bad homes.'

That sounded a reasonable remark. Except, as I was to find out, she didn't see me as an innocent child.

50

There are only a few pictures of Norman Donaldson that remain in my memory. What can I remember about him? Very little, I would say. He was just a meek-looking man, who nearly always wore a suit (he had some sort of office job and often carried on working in his small study when he came home). He never seemed to disagree with his wife.

'Yes, dear,' seemed to be his most common remark to her.

And what did he say to Michael and me apart from 'Good morning', 'Goodnight' and 'Are you ready?'? I suppose a little more than that, but that's all I can recall now.

How I wish I could say the same about his wife.

There are times even now when unwanted images of her come uninvited into my mind, bringing back memories of the day when I was to see the person she really was. One who just about snarled at me when she finally let me know her true feelings about me and the reasons why she had brought me into her home. It's a memory I can never erase because this was a day that led to a day-long nightmare, a nightmare that lasted for four years. Even now it makes me shudder to think of how she had calculated all the stages of her plans which would result in her having complete control over me. Her first step was to make me feel powerless so that within a short time I would not have enough strength left to defy her.

She certainly didn't rush it – it must have taken nearly a year to get what she wanted. Her first small success came after the social workers had ceased their visits, when she made me believe that legal papers had been signed by both parties. That meant, she explained, that I was to live in her house until I was eighteen. In other words, should I decide I wasn't happy there, it was too late for me to ask to return to the home. Not that this was true, but sadly for me, I believed what she said and didn't think to question it.

Not that I wanted to leave my brother, not then – although a few months later I did. I simply dreamt of escaping that house but by then Mrs Donaldson had subtly placed beliefs in my head that there was nowhere else I could go and no one I could confide in.

'The social workers are so pleased you two have settled in' was one of her remarks often repeated to Michael and me, but I knew it was said for me to absorb. As was, 'They think it's remarkable how Michael has adjusted so well to being here.' And a few more comments like that that made Michael beam as I tried hard to force myself to do the same.

I was too young to realise then just how determined this woman was to weaken the bond between my brother and me. She worked hard at loosening it a fraction every single day.

And when did I know that it no longer existed?

When my brother made it clear to me.

* * *

What shocked me about Michael to begin with happened after the shopping spree when all his school clothes were replaced. He said something in front of me that I could hardly believe I had heard correctly. It was the Saturday morning before we started at our new school when he told Mrs Donaldson that he had decided which name to use.

'I like the one you suggested, Terence,' he told her, 'and I'll be called Terry, won't I?'

What a beaming smile he received from her in return.

'That's good, Terry,' she said, making them both laugh together while my eyes must have widened with shock.

'Why are you calling yourself that?' I asked him.

'Well, now my surname's Donaldson, we thought it would be nice for me to have a whole new name. Don't you see, Gerri?' was his rather smug answer.

'Is my name going to be changed as well?' I asked.

'No, Gerri, we've decided you can keep yours,' Mrs Donaldson told me. Not that she explained why that was and I didn't think to question it because I was pleased that I was not losing the name and surname that linked me to Ma. At least that was until I found out the reason my name was not being changed.

What I had no idea of then was now my brother had changed his name, he was no longer going to say that I was his sister.

'It just looks odd if we have different surnames,' was his excuse.

That was the beginning of our second disturbing conversation. The first one, which I can remember just about every word of, was about my relationship with Emily Donaldson.

It was after I had done something that annoyed her. I can't remember what it was now because the slightest thing made her turn harshly on me, or so it seemed. Michael was in the kitchen when it happened. I looked sideways, trying to catch his eye when he must have heard me being spoken to with a voice loaded with contempt. I was hoping to get a thumbs up or at least one of his smiles, which would have sent me the message that he was on my side.

Surely he must have noticed that there was little if any affection coming in my direction? By then it felt more like dislike than simple annoyance. It made me feel worn down and I needed my brother to act as though he was on my side for I had no idea why she felt so angry with me. But to my surprise, instead of looking annoyed by her remarks, he just avoided looking at me.

It must be because he doesn't want to upset her, was one of the many excuses I kept making for him. At least that helped me feel a little better until I was on my own with him and we talked about it.

'Well, maybe you should have a think about what

you've done to annoy her,' was his cold response. But he didn't leave it there; instead he just about scowled at me. 'Gerri, are you playing that old game of making me feel we made a mistake being here? I suppose you're just jealous because I'm adopted and you're not.'

I gulped at that – I hadn't known.

'What do you mean?' was all I could manage to say.

'I'm their son now. That's what I mean, so don't insult them. I like it here. So, you'd better stop trying to cause trouble between us or I'll stop speaking to you.'

With that, he squared his shoulders and with his head held high, walked off, leaving me puzzled, hurt and also depressed. I didn't understand what had made him sound angry with me, that knowledge came later. As far as I could see, there wasn't anything I had done wrong.

51

If that wasn't bad enough, finding out from the very first day that we went to our new school that no one seemed to believe we came from the same family was worse. I remember saying to one of the girls in my class that Michael was my brother, only to get a strange look before she walked off. I then saw her whispering away to a couple of other girls who kept looking over in my direction and I knew they were talking about me.

I kept quiet after that.

Mrs Donaldson made sure my school clothes were spotless and without creases, but they were also rather shabby. During those years we went to the same school, Michael (who I could not bring myself to call Terry) with his thick dark hair cut into a neat style, his dark blue blazer and well-fitting grey flannel trousers always looked exceptionally smart. And I do remember clearly how he reacted when I brought up the fact that us having different surnames was difficult, or at least it was for me.

'I mean, don't people ask questions about it?'

'So don't go around telling people I'm your brother,' he abruptly told me. 'It makes you look stupid.'

I waited for him to laugh and pat my arm, which would tell me he was just teasing me, but there was no friendly smile on his face and none of his old bursts of spontaneous laughter either, which made me realise he meant every word. Though I did get the feeling he felt sorry for me when he added more softly, 'Anyhow, it's a good thing we don't look alike, isn't it?' Then he smiled at me and for just a few seconds I felt I was looking into the eyes of someone else: they were the eyes of my father, I realised. For some reason that made me shiver a little.

He was right: our colouring was completely different. With his dark hair and hazel eyes, Michael had taken after our father's side of the family, whereas my dark-blonde hair and blue eyes was from Ma's side. So, no, we were not that similar. As we grew older and his skinny frame shot up in height and filled out, I remained fairly small. I would say that by the time we were teenagers there was no resemblance at all.

During those four years we were both under the Donaldsons' roof, I felt that all my brother's memories of our early years dissolved, as did his affection for me.

That was the first stage of Emily Donaldson's plan and it had succeeded.

Even at school we were rarely seen together, which can hardly be blamed on the fact that we were in different classes. As all the pupils had their breaks at the same time, I expected us to sit together sometimes, but we never did.

Instead, within a few weeks of being there, Michael had become one of a tight group of friends and remained so throughout the time I was there. He certainly had the ability to make friends quickly, I thought miserably, for I hadn't.

My brother was invited to parties which pleased the Donaldsons, while I never was. I can still remember how I tried to work out why that was. After all, I had been popular in both the previous schools I had been to, but not this one. It was not that anyone was nasty to me, it was just that none of the class tried to chat with me on our breaks, far less invite me to their homes. After that, and I still don't know why really, I kept quiet about our relationship. It was as if all the confidence I had while in the home had been drained out of me.

What I didn't know then was the reason that kept the girls in my class away from me and the teachers watchful. But I do know now.

52

When did everything change? It transformed from being rather boring into something that had the whiff of evil lurking in the air. I sensed this shift in atmosphere almost every day from the start of the six-week-long summer holidays. With the number of tears that I shed in that period, my pillow must have been wringing wet every single night – I made sure to cry without a noise.

As the final bell sounded to announce school was out, was I the only pupil not running off laughing and cheering that they were free from classes for the rest of that summer? I suspect I was, for I could not share that joy, even though my brother certainly did.

Ever since I sent my very first letter to Holly, I had not given up hope that she would contact me, for hadn't she promised that we would meet again during these holidays? I had dreamt I would be on that ferry as soon as the term ended; I so wanted to see a letter coming through the letter box addressed to me. But as the months stretched by, there was not a letter or even a postcard for me. It was not until the last day of school that my dwindling hope finally evaporated to be replaced with a feeling of abject misery. When I sat in the classroom on the last day of that term, all I could think about was that I was never going to go to England, perhaps I would never see Holly and her uncle again and the few weeks of freedom away from the Donaldsons that I so yearned for were not to be. All my excitement about making that journey had been a complete waste of time.

Stop thinking of a trip you'll never make, I told myself fiercely, just about holding back the tears of disappointment that pricked my eyes.

One day you will, said the voice confidently.

How, Ma?

I only know that one day everything will turn out all right.

When I asked when that would be, I could hear only silence and so I knew that Ma was no longer there. Not knowing what the future held for me made me even more apprehensive.

It only took a couple of days to realise that Emily Donaldson seemed to find my unhappiness amusing. I might have tried to put on a brave face, but I hadn't managed to fool her. I'm sure she could tell that seeing my brother so excited and getting ready for his holiday with two of his new friends and their parents made me feel even worse. They were going to spend two weeks in Portrush, a popular seaside town in County Antrim that even I had heard of, but never visited. And watching him being collected hardly raised my spirits either. Being left alone with only Mrs Donaldson for company was just about the worst thing I could think of.

With my brother having distanced himself from me, and not hearing from Holly, I was beginning to feel both isolated and scared. There really was something frightening about that woman. Once Michael had left, those sharp, bright eyes of hers met mine more than once, giving me the uneasy feeling that she had something planned which I was not going to like.

I even missed seeing the lady from social services. Their visits had stopped several months earlier, which made me feel that there was no one left who was on my side. I had sent Jessica at the home a letter saying it was nice where I was but I missed her and everyone there. I never received a reply, which came as a surprise. Later, I would learn the reason for this. Anyway, it seemed now that Michael was already formally adopted, social services felt further visits to check on me were not necessary, a piece of news which Mrs Donaldson could hardly wait to impart. Even that gleeful announcement would have a reason and I found out what it was later on that week.

'What do you think about sinners?' she suddenly asked me when I was still finishing my breakfast.

'I don't really think about them,' was my answer. After all, I was hardly of an age to give the subject much consideration.

'Well, I do – a lot. And I believe they should be punished for their crimes. Now don't you agree with me there?'

As I didn't understand what she was getting at, I must have looked up at her blankly.

'I can see that your opinion must be different from mine, but that's what I would have expected of you. You see, Gerri, I believe those who commit unpardonable sins should be punished for then – and not mildly either. Until they sincerely repent, they must suffer until the life they have created for themselves is hardly worth living. And that takes time, a great deal of it.'

Is she crazy? was the question that came to mind.

Be careful, darlin'.

Of course I hadn't a clue what Emily Donaldson was talking about, although I could tell she meant every single word. There was such a cold glimmer in her eyes, that twinges of fear were coursing through me. It took another couple of years for me to learn in my history classes what excuses religious fanatics make to justify their actions. Had I studied the subject that much earlier, I might have worked out what I was facing.

Little wonder I felt cold shivers crawling up my spine.

I might not have understood what she was talking about, but I could feel that suppressed dislike of me coming in my direction. Unfortunately, none of us – Matron, Jessica or the social workers – had any idea that Emily Donaldson knew just about all the details of our family's scandal. Within a matter of hours, news of what had happened had swept through the village we lived in and to the surrounding villages, one of which the Donaldsons inhabited. How the locals worked out certain parts of what had taken place,

I don't know. It seems there is always someone who can't resist letting out the details of, in this case a crime, that for the children's sake was meant to be covered up.

If only the social workers had been made aware of the extent of Emily Donaldson's knowledge, maybe they would have questioned the couple more on their reasons for taking me into their care. The fact that they wanted to adopt my brother but only foster me really should have raised some suspicions.

53

That morning as I munched on my toast, little did I realise that I was minutes from learning why I was in the Donaldsons' home. Now that Emily Donaldson had me all to herself, she was determined to make me tell her everything I knew about what had taken place in my home. She wanted me to realise as quickly as possible that the sinners she was talking about were my mother and me. Ma might have left the world, but I hadn't. Which meant she only had me to admit my sins and make me repent – in her opinion that was the duty of a good Christian.

Did she know that there was a barrier in my mind that had protected me for over two years from accessing those disturbing memories? I believe she did, but that didn't stop her being the one who over just a matter of days managed to start pulling it down. Once it began to crumble, I saw some of the darkness of my past, which took away any peace I had in my life.

How did she do it? By telling me some of the details she had heard about. The sound of the ambulance's siren as it arrived in the village was the first fact she threw at me. That made me picture the feel of that stretcher beneath me when I was carried into the waiting vehicle. Yes, I had also heard the wailing of the siren and I could sense that although I couldn't see her, Ma was with me.

I was, darlin'.

The next remark was, 'I have a friend who lived very near to where your family used to be and there's nothing she's not told me. She never liked any of you, she said there wasn't a religious bone in either of your parents' bodies.'

My mouth was gaping with shock. But shock or not, it made me feel angry. What right did she have to insult my family?

None, my darlin', but remember I said for you to be careful. Think before you answer. Don't give her anything to use against you.

Seeing this barbed remark had struck home made her give a nasty smirk of satisfaction. 'Little wonder you never wanted to go back there, is it, Gerri? Even that friend of your mother's – Maureen, isn't it? – said she couldn't have you in her house. You know that's true, don't you?'

'No, it's not,' I managed to say, summoning up my courage to protect Maureen. But then I remembered how I had wanted to go and stay with her family where my little brothers were, but she never suggested it. And she hadn't visited us once in the home since the day she took us there. I had to bite my tongue not to let Mrs Donaldson see she had struck a nerve.

I could feel my cheeks burning with rage at everything

she seemed to want to hurl at me. 'I did want to go and see my little brothers and all my friends. I couldn't though, because I was too ill. That's why,' I told her indignantly, tears of frustration pricking behind my eyes.

'Mmm … don't try and fool me, you know that no one there would want to see your face in the town ever again. And no mother would want you mixing with their children. The school would have had to expel you; not one teacher would have wanted you in their classroom. And teachers might have tried to stop the children talking, but they knew about you and the utter shame you and your mother had brought to your family.

'And your poor brother, what he must have gone through, being kept away from school because of your depravity.'

With that unpleasant smirk on her face, she paused for a moment, no doubt hoping for the enormity of her words to sink in. Maybe she was expecting me to butt in, so she could goad me further.

Don't! That will only please her.

I won't, Ma.

Instead I looked down at my hands, trying to keep my expression emotionless, which only irritated her. Not that it stopped her from carrying on, as her venom was released to fill the silence.

'Well, I can tell you that if he had gone back to school after the holidays, your brother would have heard about all the bad things you and your mother had done. I'm sure you know how good children are at eavesdropping. He would have found out all the terrible details from his classmates so that's why he missed a whole term of his education. At least that Maureen made sure he didn't go back there, just put him in the home with you. Though I suppose that was down to your father. And what was the worst thing he did? Made sure his innocent little son was tied to his delinquent daughter. And now I've got you in *my* home, which hardly makes me happy, I can tell you.'

I wanted to ask her why she had brought me there, but my mind seemed to have taken away my capacity to speak. By now though, it seemed there was nothing that could stop her.

'I see you're not asking why the teachers wouldn't have you in their classrooms, but I suppose you know why. They would be scared you might open that mouth of yours and tell other children nasty, dirty things.'

'I wouldn't do that,' I managed to say.

'What?! You didn't want anyone to know what your father and you were doing? I know what you did, Gerri, my friend told me all about it. You slept with him, didn't you? Your own father!'

And that, I know now, was what she had been working up to. I can remember the triumph in her voice when she spat the words out in disgust. I was so completely shocked at such an accusation that I must have looked dazed; I can remember words of denial stuck in my throat and all I could do was shake my head in disbelief.

'Oh, there you go again, Gerri, saying nothing happened. But then you don't know the meaning of truth, do you?

You're just a compulsive liar – have been since you were able to string a sentence together, I would think. So sad for your brother, having you as a sister, though that's come to an end.'

What did she mean? But I was in shock and could only look at her with my mouth gaping.

She just wants to upset you so just keep on saying nothing, Ma told me again.

'Your brother is such a good boy, so well mannered, so attentive. I decided from the moment I met him that I had to do something to stop you destroying his life,' she continued.

What a bitch were the words that entered my head, which made me want to pick up anything near to hand and hurl it at her. No doubt she wanted me to explode with rage and then she would have another excuse to punish me. I knew not to give her that opportunity. Instead I clenched my fists tightly under the table and forced myself to keep both still and silent. Not that my silence made her stop. After giving me another cold stare, she carried on: 'Thank goodness your brother's managed to get a life without you in it here. He's not reliant on you anymore, is he? Oh no, he's made some decent friends and he's doing well at school and regaining the confidence that you tried to take away from him.

'It was him who saw how often you wanted to be alone with your father and wasn't he sent out of the house all the time to that friend of your mother's when all he wanted was to stay in his own home? So that tells me everything. Both my husband and I decided immediately he would be our son and now the adoption has been finalised. And you? You're only ever going to be a foster child, one without any family. We don't want you here a moment longer than necessary. You thought we would adopt you too, didn't you?'

And as she spat that last barb out, she laughed derisively in my face.

54

It wasn't as though I even wanted to be adopted – well, not by Emily Donaldson anyhow – although she made me question just who did I have left in my life? The answer to that was absolutely no one. Even Holly appeared to have abandoned me and my letter to Jessica at the home remained unanswered, so I believed there was not one person who wished to be close to me.

Judging by the almost gloating expression on Emily Donaldson's face, she must have felt those efforts of hers to unnerve me were working. I could tell she was pleased with herself when those thin colourless lips of hers turned up into a mocking smile: 'Now don't look so worried, dear,' I heard her say as she patted my shoulder. Glancing down at that wrinkled hand, I was so tempted to shrug it off. Luckily a few crumbs of common sense had told me not to. No doubt she felt me stiffen at her touch. I expect she believed it was the beginning of me fearing her, and knowing that would have pleased her.

'Oh, cheer up for goodness' sake, Gerri! We don't want

to have to look at such a doleful face. I'm not some cold-hearted woman who doesn't think of your future. Just because I know all about you doesn't mean that you won't be looked after.'

It was the first time she had said anything like that. Without thinking, I looked up at her and asked what she meant. Her hand gripped my shoulder more tightly. 'I'm sure you know what I mean,' she said and before I could tell her I didn't, she began talking about some plans she had.

'Now, I'm going to show you what I've done to help make you more independent, Gerri. It's important that both you and Terry are in charge of your own lives so don't sit there looking at me with your mouth open. Get off that chair now and follow me. There's something I want you to see,' she said firmly.

As I slithered off the chair, I was rather puzzled when, without a backward glance, she walked towards the door that led down a few steps to part of the building that had once been a garage. It was now used as a storage room for gardening tools and the large lawn mower. I couldn't imagine how anything in there would be interesting or could better my life in any way. Well, I was still a little naive then. I had only been in that place a couple of times when Michael and I watched the gardener taking out the lawn mower. Not long before we came to live there, another, bigger garage that could house two cars had been built. I can remember that it was a dusty and dark place, with oil streaks spattered on the cement floor. My nose had twitched when we walked in and I suppose it was that musty air that had gone up it, making me sneeze and then start coughing.

It was the moment when she turned on the light that I suddenly felt a sickening surge of dread. She led the way down the two steps into that garage, into what I saw as a nightmare. Because instead of standing in the middle of a large almost empty space, we were now in a small part that had been sectioned off with corrugated iron panels.

Far worse though was what was there. My eyes blinked in disbelief at what I saw. *This can't be what she has planned*, I said to myself when my eyes focused on three objects: a narrow single bed, a small desk and a straight-backed wooden chair, which was placed in front of it. Dazed, I slowed down, turned my head around and found myself looking at some hooks screwed into a piece of wood and then fixed to the brick wall behind me. I could feel my legs shaking as my inner voice screamed silently, *NO!*

Try not to show any reaction, darlin'.

I'll do my best, Ma.

But trying didn't stop my legs from continuing to shake.

'Here's the little surprise I said I had for you, Gerri. Something that will help you get more independent,' Emily Donaldson said smugly. 'A room of your own. You can see how much work has been done to make you comfortable here. You see we've blocked off the sight of all the gardening gear. Wouldn't want to go to sleep seeing that mess now, would you?'

That was not a question I could bring myself to answer any more than I could say anything about the following remarks she made.

'We decided this would be best for both you and Terry. Our son will keep his own room and now he'll even be able to have friends stay over in the room next to him.'

My room, I realised she meant. Only, she was making it clear that it no longer was my room.

'You should be looking a little grateful, having this part all to yourself. It means you have your own space and Terry will have his.'

How I cringed each time she called Michael that. *He's Ma's son, not yours*, I wanted to yell at her.

That will only give her satisfaction.

So, I bottled the words up.

I just knew what it was she was up to then – she wanted us separated as much as possible. I tried as hard as I could not to show the horror I was feeling. This room she had created looked like a prison to me and in a way, that's what it turned out to be.

I could feel her eyes on me, searching my face, and I knew she was looking for a reaction. Was it fear she hoped to see there?

Showing how you feel will give her more power over you, whispered the voice in my ear.

I was just turning ten, so I suppose it was hardly surprising that I hadn't managed to toughen up enough to stand up for myself a little more, but I did my best.

'You can see I'm not heartless, Gerri. Have another look

around you. There's a nice bed for you and I've put in a lamp so you can do your homework on the desk.'

'But there's no daylight in here,' I managed to say. Thankfully I stopped myself from telling her that I was scared of the dark.

'No, so that's why I put in the lamp. Now sit down on the bed while I explain a few rules and if you obey them, it will make us get on much better.'

Do it, Gerri!

Of course what I wanted was to refuse but instead, with the little bit of willpower I had left, I perched on the edge of the bed. I could feel the hardness of the thin mattress under the blanket and thought this was confirmation that there was no way she wanted me to feel comfortable in there. I still hoped this was just going to be a temporary thing and that she would let me back in the house before Michael came back.

I was wrong there.

It was that hope though that made me sit still and listen to her.

'First, let's run through a few of your needs, such as ablutions. You know what that word means?'

'No,' I said.

Her eyebrows raised. 'I should have known that, I suppose. It means washing, keeping yourself clean. As for baths, you can have a shower once a week. If you look behind you, you can see a wooden seat – that's the lid on the chemical lavatory I've had brought in for you. Now, what can you see near it, on that small table?'

I glanced back to where a metal bowl sat on a small round table and next to it was a plastic tumbler and a large plastic jug.

'And what do you think it's there for, Gerri?'

It was hardly difficult to work out what she was planning, which made me begin to feel more frightened, but I managed to sit still and listen to her.

'It's for getting yourself clean every day and making sure those hands of your hands are washed every time you use the lavatory. I'll be looking at your nails each morning when you come up to the kitchen to collect the water and your breakfast. Once a week you will strip your bed and bring the sheets and pillowcase and your towel to be washed in my washing machine and I'll give you a fresh set. The toilet paper is not to be wasted – I've placed twenty sheets there and I expect them to last for two weeks. Now do you understand your routine? Don't want to be making mistakes, do we?'

I didn't. What she was telling me was more than I could take in. Now my legs felt even more wobbly, my mind was spinning. Surely, she wasn't about to make me little more than a prisoner in her old garage, living a completely different life to my brother?

Put your shoulders back and whatever you do, don't cry, Gerri.

I bit my lip to try and stop those salty tears from coming. I'm sure by then Emily Donaldson could see that I was struggling to take in my situation and was both scared and upset – what child wouldn't have been? She did say that I would still be going to church with them on Sundays but that was the only pleasant remark she made. I suppose if she hadn't taken me, the vicar might have wondered why.

I was already shaken when she told me there were more rules.

'On weekdays you will stay here and get yourself up and get ready for school. Understood?'

'Yes.'

'I'll show you where the bus stop is, then you can take yourself there. That's the way you will travel.'

'What about Michael, won't he be coming with me?'

'You mean Terry, and no, he won't. Either my husband or I will drive him there.'

It was that last sentence that made me buckle. This was not only separating me from my brother, it was getting me to be outside of the family. Something told me that this was not a short-term punishment, it was designed to exclude me from the only member of my family I had left. I couldn't help myself then. The tears I had fought so hard to hold back spilled from my eyes and then I couldn't stop them.

'Why are you doing this to me?' I wailed.

'I'm not doing anything to you, Gerri. We wanted to adopt Terry, but you had to come as well. Considering that I knew all about your ugly past, it was very good of me to agree to having you anywhere near my family. The only reason you were brought here is because your useless mother never loved you in the first place. If she had, she would never have killed herself and left you in this world alone.'

Darlin', don't believe one word she says.

'That's not true!' I just about screamed the words out. She had finally got through that part of me that stopped me from reacting to her cruel insults about me and my family. 'She was sick for weeks before she died.'

'No, she died the night you were taken to hospital.'

'She was with me!'

I was, my darlin'.

'Why are you saying all this?'

'Because you need to accept that it was you who caused all the harm in your family. I told you I know what you did, you and your father. It's disgusting! Which is why I don't want you living in our house. Now don't say anything more. Just come with me, get your things and bring them down here. When it's six o'clock, you can knock on the door and I'll give you your supper.'

'I won't! You're lying to me.'

'Is that so?' she said as she jumped from the chair, raised her hand high and then with all the power in her arm, she brought it down on my cheek, making me reel backwards. 'Don't you *ever* be rude to me again, Gerri, or I'll give you something far worse than that.'

A cold hatred filled my heart, a feeling that has never left.

'Now, do as I say, come with me, pack up all your clothes and books and bring them down here. If you don't apologise and do as I say, the door will be locked and you'll stay in here as long as it takes, until you say sorry.'

She means it, so say it.

So, I had to let all my pride slide away as I meekly said, 'I'm sorry, Mrs Donaldson.'

It's not true that I didn't love you, said the voice.

But it didn't say she hadn't killed herself.

55

That first night in my small partitioned-off room, I curled up and tried to sleep but I could still hear my mother's voice.

It wasn't you that was bad, it was your da. That's why I left him, but I'll never leave you.

And I felt familiar warm fingers touching mine with such love that I gained comfort.

Was I asleep? Was it all a dream? I don't know, but I kept telling myself it had to be real for that is what I clung to so desperately.

It was in that miserable room, around the time when dawn was breaking, that I became aware of a few shafts of daylight coming thorough the one tiny window. While I lay in that small hard bed, I felt a glimmer of a memory stirring. It was as though an unseen hand had pulled back the curtain in my mind just a fraction, but enough for me to know there was much more to be revealed.

You might ask why I didn't go to one of my teachers at this stage and tell them what was happening. That was what my friend Holly had done and look how she'd been helped. But the teachers were distant to me and no matter how hard I worked, there was seldom any praise coming in my direction. When there was hardly a mistake in my homework, they congratulated me politely but never with any warmth. Instinct told me I was not a child they would believe. Most probably they would just say how lucky I was to be in a home like the Donaldsons'. Not only that, they might also repeat what I had told them to Emily Donaldson and that would make my life under her roof even worse. If I ran away, which I had given serious consideration to, just where would I go? Hadn't all those little remarks during the time that I had been with the Donaldsons told me that I couldn't go back to the home? And after all, hadn't I told the social workers I was happy there? So, who exactly would believe me?

I think everyone knows the story about the frog placed in boiling water – I'm sure Emily Donaldson must have known that one too. Pop the little creature in a pan of boiling water and it springs out, but put it in cold water then gradually bring it to the boil and the poor little frog is incapable of leaping out. Or rather, it will have forgotten how to. And that's exactly where I was.

56

It was four years before I escaped from my life in that garage. Four years when Emily Donaldson controlled me. Four years when she punished me for what she called 'my sins'. Four years when she successfully turned my brother against me. And four years of me fighting not to give in to the most debilitating depression.

And let me tell you that was far from easy. How I hated being in that garage, because let's face it, that's what it was. In the summer months it was so hot and stuffy I could hardly concentrate on my homework and when winter came, there was ice on the inside of the tiny window in my poky section of the garage. At least she gave me extra bedding then and when temperatures went down to zero and below, she brought down a large stone hot water bottle. Forget the idea that this might have been kindness, in case you're thinking it was; she just didn't want me getting ill. If it was found out that I was sleeping in an unheated garage instead of the house, this might just have earned her some unpleasant criticism, especially if a doctor had to be called to the house. That would have been enough to have had a social worker winging their way there – and that was not something Emily Donaldson would have welcomed. She may not have wanted me getting ill but she did want my memories to resurface so that they would haunt me, for she believed if they did, I would blame myself for my mother's death and hate myself.

Keeping clean and tidy gave me such goosebumps as I washed in the cold water. I shivered in the chilly air of the garage and got dressed as quickly as I could. During those winter months I longed for my weekly shower. It made me feel a little better washing my hair and body in the warm centrally heated bathroom. I was allowed to do so on a Saturday because I had to look fresh and smart on the Sunday – the one day of the week when I joined the family. I was even allowed to have breakfast in the kitchen with everyone else and Michael seemed pleased to see me. He chattered away about some of his friends and things he had done at school. It was clear to me then that he did not know exactly why I had changed rooms when he was away. He believed I had wanted to be separate and I dared not say anything to contradict that. Such was his indoctrination that he would just have thought I was trying to cause trouble and he never visited me in the garage so he had no idea how I was living. I could tell he was happy with the Donaldsons, who he now, to my immense annoyance, called Mum and Dad.

After breakfast was over, I was told to change into my

Sunday outfit, the one item of mine still kept in the house. I knew why that was: Emily Donaldson didn't want it getting creased or dirty down in the garage. I was to look as smart as my brother when it came to attending church. What would the vicar and his wife have thought if the foster child looked scruffy and unkempt?

The only good thing about living in the garage was that I didn't have to keep seeing that pursed-up mouth of Emily Donaldson's whenever I encountered her. The first couple of days I was there I found that there was a part of that corrugated iron structure that I could open. Not that I knew then why it was there, I found out later when school started. It was so that she could open the garage doors and let me out so there was no more going in the house.

When it wasn't a school day, I crept through the gap into the main garage, where there was a larger window I could open. If I stood on the edge of the lawnmower, I could climb through it. At least I could go out into the sun and get fresh air. I would head for the fields and when I found a restful place, I would sit down and take out my library book. Try as I might to read, dark thoughts kept running through my head. What had Emily Donaldson meant by telling me she knew about my past and that no one would want me back in the village? It made me determined to try and remember more of my life just before I was taken into hospital. I needed to fill in those blanks for that might explain her vindictive jibes. She had so enjoyed telling me enough to make me wonder what had really happened in the house.

Those disturbing dreams were returning for the first time in months. The first one which appeared had no people in it, just shadows that looked like rain-filled clouds, floating in my mind. I could hear male voices calling my name and saying, 'We want you' and those were the words that woke me with a jolt. The second time the dream was far worse: there were the clouds again, only this time there were glittering eyes with no body or head, just dark orbs glowering down at me. Who did they belong to? was the question I asked myself when I woke shaking with fear, my pyjamas soaked in sweat.

The dreams made me feel miserable for most of the day. How I yearned for both Ma and Holly. I wanted the comfort of my mother's warm arms around me, to hear her voice gently singing my favourite songs. And Holly, who at such a young age was able to comfort me after each of my nightmares. I could still picture those nights when my screams woke me and she would talk softly, brush the damp hair from my face and tell me we all had those dreams. I thought of how close we had been and wondered why she had forgotten me despite her assurances that she would keep in touch. Sobs came from my chest and plump tears fell onto the pages of the open book that I was staring down at but not taking in the words.

Why have I lost everything, I thought, *my family and my closest friend?*

Try not to cry, darlin'. Everything will get better for you.

How, Ma?

Because people as bad as that Emily Donaldson won't get away with hurting you forever.

It was then I remembered what Ma had once said: 'It wasn't you, darlin', it was your da.'

Try as I might, I still couldn't remember what they meant, any more than I could grasp the meaning of what Emily Donaldson had said about my past. Not that I wanted to hear more about it from her, but I needed to make sense of it all.

But Emily Donaldson was certainly not concerned about my mental state. I could tell she was getting impatient that I had not remembered much about my past. She waited for about a year, when I had started at the senior school. By then I hardly saw my brother at all except for trips to church every Sunday. At this point she seemed to renew her efforts to torture me and what she said as she probed was graphic enough to make me squirm.

'So, Gerri, are you really going to tell me you can't remember what happened between you and your father?' Then, when that elicited a puzzled look from me, she tried again: 'Terry knows.'

Talk about unsubtle.

'No, I don't remember.'

'Oh, stop lying, you little whore! The whole village knew about it. You slept with him, didn't you?'

I gulped at the very thought.

'I didn't.'

'Oh, you did. No doubt when you can't lie anymore,

you're going to say he forced you. And even if he did, why didn't you tell anyone? Because you didn't tell, did you? Not your mother or that Maureen.'

I just couldn't bring myself to answer her anymore. Instead I burst into tears.

It was your da, not you who was bad were the words that I had heard in my head, words I clung to then, trying to find where they had come from. There was a feeling of all my breath leaving me as that wall that had blocked my memories for three years began to crumble. I could hear that voice of hers as, ignoring my tears, she rumbled on with her knives poking at my memory.

'So, think about it, Gerri. Why did you let Terry go to the neighbour's alone all the time?'

It was then that my mind shot back to one of those times when Da was holding my arm and telling my brother he could go but I had to stay. Why was that? I suddenly knew it was because he was waiting for someone. And then the picture of a man dressed in long black robes with a Bible in his hands floated to the fore.

'He wanted me to stay because the priest came to say prayers with us.'

She laughed then, mocking me.

'You'd better try to remember a little harder,' she said with a nasty smile. Then she turned and walked out, leaving me shaking with fear. But she didn't stop there: she could tell my memory was gradually coming back by the pallor of my face and the dark shadows that appeared like bruises under my eyes.

'Not slept well then, have you, Gerri? Your guilt giving you nightmares, is it?' she asked me mockingly the next day.

By then I couldn't hide my dislike for her any longer and just looked away. She was careful when selecting words as the weapons she used to attack me: 'Now you know why your mother killed herself – you brought such shame on her that she couldn't bring herself to live anymore' was one of her most poisonous darts. It gave me so much pain when she shot those barbs into my ears and straight into my mind.

There were quite a few more hateful phrases that she spat out when she thought I was at a particularly low ebb. Such as hearing my brother had been invited to yet another birthday party, something that never happened to me and something she never failed to highlight.

'Now you know why no one at school wants you as a friend – their mothers don't want their children mixing with any damaged ones. They would be worried all the time that nasty, filthy things would be said.'

I didn't ask her then how the parents at my school had found out what happened in a village so many miles away because I already knew: all those mothers would be thinking Emily Donaldson must be a saint to foster a damaged child like me. Still, despite all her hints and snippets of information, not all my memories had come back. But I now remembered those initial acts that my father had carried out on me and how I had hated them; that part of the wall was down. I also had a clear picture in my head of Da telling Michael he must go to Maureen's. My brother might have told his adopted mother that he hadn't wanted to go, though most likely she had twisted those facts. But on this, I had a full recollection – he could hardly wait to get away.

57

Now I sometimes wonder what would have happened to me if I hadn't gone to the church services with the Donaldsons and my brother every Sunday. I can remember how quite often sadness overwhelmed me and I wished I could die. I'm pretty sure now that if Emily Donaldson had left sleeping pills where I could find them, I would have swallowed them in an instant. Then I would be with my mother, wouldn't I? For she might not have been in this world but, wherever she was, I felt she still loved me. And that belief was what kept me from taking notice of everything I was told – I clung to the knowledge that my mother had loved me and still did.

The one person who saved me from entering a complete depression was the vicar. I'm convinced now that he knew why I was fostered, but not how I was being treated. Having heard that only my brother had been adopted, though, must have told him that I was hardly a loved child and that all the Donaldsons were doing in keeping me was their Christian duty. He and his wife must have talked about it and decided that my brother having a different surname from me would surely be upsetting for me. I doubt that he approved of that, especially as Michael was the only member of my family I had left. I would think that the vicar and his wife's understanding of Christian duty was very different to Emily Donaldson's. As I got to know them better, I realised that they wanted to help those in need and had decided that I was a suitable candidate. They must have worked out the extent of the interest they could take in me that my foster mother could hardly argue with.

I was both surprised and pleased when after church one Sunday the vicar approached the Donaldsons and thanked them for coming to the service and bringing my brother and me with them. And then he began to talk to them about me.

'I heard her voice when she sang one of the hymns,' he told them. 'What a lovely clear voice she has. I would like her to join the choir – if she would like to, that is.'

Before Emily Donaldson could come up with a reason why that would be difficult, I managed to say that I would absolutely love to – 'Our mother was a really good singer, wasn't she?' I said, turning towards Michael.

'She was,' he agreed, without thinking that it might annoy Emily Donaldson. I could tell that this was the last thing the Donaldsons wanted, but being a woman who made sure that everyone, especially the vicar, respected her for being a devout Christian, this put Emily in a difficult position: she could hardly refuse his request.

'Yes, of course, Vicar,' she told him and my heart

fluttered when I heard him tell her that choir practice took place twice a week. 'And don't worry about her homework, be better if she comes straight here as the bus stops almost outside the vicarage. That will save time and she can have her tea with us before joining the other children for choir practice.'

Now that was hardly what Emily Donaldson expected. In her mind she had wanted to take me there, say a friendly goodbye and ask what time to collect me. She certainly didn't want the vicar and his wife to become so friendly with me.

Did she show me how annoyed she was with that invite? Yes, she certainly did.

She called me some more bad names – in my innocence I had to look up 'whore' and 'strumpet' in my dictionary to understand what she meant. Even the vicar's invitation for me to join the choir was used: 'He'd better not find out what a little whore you really are or he won't want you mixing with the other young choristers, will he?'

Then there were the threats of what would happen to me if she heard I was running her down. Threats that let me know she might just send me away. Not to the home I had been to, but to a place where disobedient children were locked up. Unfortunately, I was too naive to know it was a load of nonsense.

I can remember the first time I went to the vicarage after school. It was Isabella, the vicar's wife, a pretty, rather plump, blonde-haired woman with a warm and welcoming smile, who gently asked me a few questions. To begin with they were about the home and then just a couple about my life with the Donaldsons – I knew she was digging a little to find out if I was happy with them.

'She's a bit strict' was all I admitted, as I thought of how that cane had landed on the backs of my legs the night before – a warning to keep my mouth shut.

'I expect she's a good cook,' Isabella said once we had finished a hearty meal which clearly I had enjoyed every mouthful of. It might have been a subtle question, but I realised later it was because she wanted to know if I was being fed well.

When summer came, I didn't look as though I spent much time in the sun.

'You look rather pale,' she observed.

That was the summer that Emily Donaldson had me working as a cleaner in her house – scrubbing floors, polishing silver, cleaning toilets and anything else menial she could find for me to do.

'Must be the good sun cream I use,' I answered.

By then I was far too scared of the Donaldsons to tell her what really happened there.

She gave me a doubtful look.

'Gerri, if ever you want to talk to anyone, my husband and I are always happy to sit down and listen to you,' she told me.

But I never did find the courage to tell them. I think they knew that Michael was the favourite and I was not given much affection. A couple of years later I found out that they had learnt a few things from the school, such as hearing there were bruises on me that the teachers were not happy about. They never did let me know that it was they who contacted the social workers and told them that they had every reason to be worried about me.

That one concerned phone call from the vicar was enough to make the social workers visit again. What they did afterwards was to report that they remained worried about me and so a few more visits from social services occurred, often unannounced. Luckily for the Donaldsons, they never asked to see my room or things would have unravelled.

But even so, they were visits that enraged Emily Donaldson.

'Have you been talking about us?' she bellowed once they drove off one day.

'No,' I told her as I saw her hand raise to land hard on the back of my head.

Whatever the vicar and his wife must have been thinking, every Sunday they put on friendly faces and greeted my foster parents with smiles. They told them they were pleased to see them and that they felt lucky to have me in the choir.

I was so grateful that twice a week I had some freedom and some normality in a warm and welcoming family. Not only that, but the people in the choir were also friendly to me and I enjoyed the singing so much. Someone once told me that if you are depressed, singing really lifts the spirits. It certainly did mine and I was over the moon when the vicar had me singing a solo of 'Silent Night' at the

Christmas Eve service. That made me feel proud and even Michael complimented me. But not Emily Donaldson, who with two red spots on her cheeks, could hardly control her fury at me being the centre of attention.

I would say now that it was the vicar and his wife who helped me get through those miserable years of being with the Donaldsons. Their involvement in my wellbeing also reduced Emily Donaldson's cruelty to me, for the social workers had once spotted bruises on me – she told them I had tried to climb a tree and fallen. But even she knew it was better that no one ever saw marks on me again. She still had her ways of making me suffer and her hatred was palpable.

58

There came a time, I suppose it must have been when I was around thirteen, when I realised that so many of my more disturbing dreams were doing their best to show me the truth about what had happened during my early years. It took me a while to slowly accept they were not just dreams, but the inner workings of my mind, finally allowing parts of my story to surface and become clearer to me. Step by step, every time I woke up I began to accept that what I once felt was just a random nightmare was far more. For the pictures were from behind that wall that I had protected myself with, when I was too young to cope with the facts of what they had done to me.

Years later, when I felt my past was seriously jeopardising my future, I decided I needed to seek professional help. Every Wednesday afternoon at 3 p.m. for many weeks, I spent an hour with my therapist. She managed to help me understand some of the difficulties that those memories of the horrors I had gone through had given me. *Why can't I just put it behind me?* was my continuous question. Hadn't

I moved on long ago and built a life I liked? I had friends who cared for me and a job I loved so why did I keep letting my mind take me back into my past? I desperately needed answers to why my dreams were still haunted and why I woke screaming and bathed in sweat on far too many occasions.

'Let's see if this analogy will help you understand it a little more, Gerri,' she said. 'Now, think of a house that looks perfect but what the happy buyer never sees is the damage to its foundations that were caused right from the very beginning when it was being built. And no matter how good the house looks, the day will finally come when the structural damage shows.'

'And what do they do to repair it?'

'Visible damage to the bricks and mortar when the foundations are not built correctly can be superficially repaired but their weakness will show, should there be a violent storm or a flood. Those events cause it to shake frighteningly and some walls start cracking and even collapsing.'

'So, what happens then?'

'Structural surveyors are called in by the insurance company and the house is declared unfit to live in and dangerous.'

'And then?'

'Then it's demolished until it turns into a pile of rubble. You see, a house's real strength lies in the quality of the foundations. Humans have a mind that can be stronger than a house, strong enough to build a new foundation but only if the person is determined enough to do that and seeks the right help, just as you have, Gerri. Sadly, some people never try – instead they seek comfort in various other things. Some drink to excess, others take drugs, while there are some who look through the bars of the prison they have been sent to and blame their past for their crimes.'

Our eyes met and in her warm brown gaze I saw both compassion and a warning.

'I think I understand,' I said. 'You mean it's up to me to build a new foundation over my past and not to use it as an excuse for all my mistakes?'

'Yes, I've only told you this because I believe you are much stronger than you realise.'

'So, what's the best way to do as you suggest?'

'You talk to me, Gerri. No matter how hard it is, tell me everything you can remember. All the hurt and the pain. Spill it out – everything you say in here is confidential, remember that. Then, once you've got it all out, you will find that as your mind begins to heal, you will place your past firmly behind you. Then you can start to make even more plans for your future and fulfil your dreams in the knowledge that you will be able to cope with whatever life throws at you.'

I so wished I had met her long ago when those haunting dreams were first coming into my sleep, making me fearful in my waking life and of what would happen the following night. She would have helped make everything so much easier.

As a child I tried my best to handle those parts of my story that forced their way into my consciousness. Part of me wanted to see them, for I had been aware for some time that there were still memory gaps. I think I had known deep down that ever since my first dream, my past was sending me a message.

So, can I remember the first time it happened? It was when I was in the home and Holly came to my bed to comfort me, remember that? And there was that dark figure in the dream – 'You know who I am, Gerri,' he said as he slid through the door and disappeared into the shadows. I knew even when I spent those years in Emily Donaldson's garage that I needed to find a way to stop my past upsetting me so much. I had to summon up enough courage to deal with her and I was determined she was not going to win. Not that I had a clue how I was going to manage that.

You will, darlin', you will. It won't be long now before you have the strength to put a stop to her and all her nonsense.

The voice brought comfort to me every time I started to panic.

What won't be long, Ma? I asked, desperate for some sort of sign.

No answer came.

But the voice made me get off my bed and go and look at the calendar on the wall, the one I had made for myself. It started on the day I had been moved into the garage and I could count the total number of months remaining before I turned eighteen, for wasn't that the age I had to be before I could leave the Donaldsons? But looking at it never cheered me up, instead it made my heart sink.

Tell me, Ma, when it will be. I'm not even halfway to being able to leave, I appealed to her in desperation.

It won't be that long, darlin'.

There were times when I even thought of joining Ma. But when I was in that mood, I realised there was no medication in the room that could help me leave my world gently, drifting off as she had done. I did in desperation study the bottle of weed killer with all its lethal warnings that sat on a high shelf in the main garage, but I was too terrified of dying in the agonising pain that the writing on the bottle described in graphic detail.

The one question that I couldn't find the answer to was did Emily Donaldson know everything that had happened, or only part of it? Whatever it was, she was not going to help me by telling me everything. Much later, when I knew the whole story, I knew she would not have wanted to believe there had been a guilty priest there.

I tried to picture all the details that appeared in the many dreams that had visited me in the home but my memory of them had faded. It was as though the people in them had done their best to erase themselves from my mind. But then I suppose I was only ten when I left, so that was hardly surprising.

At thirteen, I needed to know more.

Come back, I asked my earliest dreams, *then I will know what you were trying to tell me.*

Eventually the dream I wished for did return. It was a

dream, wasn't it? I had to ask myself that question because I felt I was fully awake when I saw a faint figure floating in the air above my head. My scalp tingled, my heart knocked against my ribs and as I lay there, I was paralysed with fear. As the figure rose higher, dark robes fell in swathes of black fabric until they nearly brushed against my face.

You know, a deep, masculine voice said. I was convinced it was a voice I had heard before, a long time ago. *You know*, it whispered again, just as it had done before. Then it slithered through the metal sheeting of my room and disappeared from sight.

My breath was fast and shallow as I sat up in bed. Seizing hold of the flex, I turned the light on. I remember my heart was pounding and my head swimming as I slumped against those metal rails of the bedhead and peered around the room but the only shadow on the wall was mine: the room was empty. It was then that I knew who the other person was: he was the one who had destroyed our family.

Now you know, darlin'. It wasn't only your da who hurt you.

No, it wasn't, I realised, but my father had welcomed the evil within himself. Even worse, he invited a greater evil into our home. How I wished there was someone I could talk to at that time – there were still so many questions running through my head that I needed the answers to.

Had my mother really killed herself as Emily Donaldson had said and if so, why?

And was it true my father didn't want any of us to live with him? Not that I wanted live with him again, although

I had once wished we could. But if the priest was no longer there, at least I would have all my brothers with me.

And Maureen, I thought, she had loved me. So, what had happened to make her walk away from us?

It was to take another three years for me to get all the answers to those questions.

59

I was fourteen when I discovered why I had never heard back from Holly. It was her uncle – who told me to drop the 'uncle' and start calling him John – who, with his warm Irish brogue and broad smile, had worked out the reason. I was both angry and tearful when it was spelt out to me and his voice might have been sympathetic, but I could tell he felt the same fury towards Emily Donaldson as I did.

Not only had she thrown all of my letters in the bin after reading them, but she also blocked all Holly's letters from reaching me. Evidently, they had been sent to the home and then forwarded to my foster mother.

If John hadn't brought Holly with him when he was visiting old friends in Ireland, I doubt she and I would ever have met again. Nor would he have bothered looking me up, had he travelled on his own. It was only because his niece begged him to find me that he had called the home, only to be told that I had left. I asked him later why he hadn't gone to Emily Donaldson's house first before coming to the school.

'I don't know really. Some instinct told me it might be better to find you there first. So, I asked Matron which school you were at when I made that call and do you know what she said, Gerri?'

'No.'

'That you would be so happy to see Holly again and she mentioned that the day you were going to the Donaldsons, you told her you were going to write a long letter to Holly. That's when I asked her if the letters Holly sent were forwarded. Turns out your foster mother wanted them sent on but addressed to her, so she could give them to you when you returned from school. And that was when I asked for the name of the school you were at. Holly wanted to know why you had suddenly stopped writing to her, she was so worried about you. So, Gerri, it was she who pushed me into looking for you. I still wasn't sure if it was a good idea but she had begged and begged me so I came here and came to see the head. 'That picture will stay in my head for a long time,' I told him. 'I could hardly believe it when the head came to fetch me out of class. When he gave me your name and asked if I knew you, I must have looked blank until he added that I might have forgotten you, but not your niece, Holly. You know, I almost burst into tears then. I still had such a lump in my throat when I saw you.'

'Because you wanted to see Holly?'

'Yes.'

That day was about the first one in the last four years when I felt happy. I just about jumped with joy at the thought of seeing John and his niece again when I followed the head into his study. The moment I went in, I recognised John straight away – four years hadn't changed him much. Not that I told him that to begin with, instead I just blurted out, 'Where's Holly?'

'Oh, she's just with some friends of mine but she's so excited to see you again.'

I thought Holly's Uncle John looked rather stern when he told me how Holly had kept asking him to find me – 'I did wonder if you had forgotten her because there were never any letters from you.'

'No, of course I never forgot her. I would never do that, she's my only friend,' I managed to say, still unaware why she hadn't received them.

'I have to tell you she was beside herself for quite a while when you never wrote back to her.'

'But I did. I wrote at least once a week and she never wrote back either – I was so worried she had forgotten me.'

I think by the expression on my face he came to his own conclusion as to what had happened to those letters, not that he said anything then. And that's when I began to realise the truth of what must have happened, which even I found hard to believe.

'Where were they sent to?' I asked.

'To the home and then, when we arrived here, we called them to see what was happening. We were given the address of the home where you and your brother now live.'

I must have snorted a bit then for I could hardly call that house a home. All the mornings I had tried to rush to the door when I heard the postman posting letters through the letter box but always Emily Donaldson almost pushed me aside to get there first and then smugly told me there was nothing for me.

'Mrs Donaldson must have stopped me from seeing them,' I said mournfully.

For a moment he looked puzzled, then asked why she would have done that.

'Because she hates me. She thinks I'm evil.'

I knew I should have kept my mouth shut as soon as I saw a slightly wary expression cross his face. He was kind enough to change the subject quickly and said that the headteacher had told him that I was doing very well at school. I nearly blurted out what came into my mind, that with everything that had gone so wrong where I lived, it was a miracle that I was able to achieve more than the basics. Instead, I bit my lip and remained silent. The bell went, indicating that I needed to get to my next class and whatever thoughts went through his mind, he told me he would be waiting for me outside the gates when school was over.

'I'll wait for you to finish. It's a dark blue Ford and I'll be parked outside the gates. We can go to that little coffee shop nearby. Is that all right with you?'

'Yes, of course, but when will I see Holly?' Tears were forming in my eyes and I could hear the desperation in my voice.

'After we've talked,' he said.

'Mrs Donaldson will be so angry if I'm late coming back.'

He gave me another look and I could see a spark of anger in it.

'Give me her number and I'll explain why you'll be a little late,' he said. 'I'll be driving you back, so it'll be quicker than the bus, won't it?'

I thought he must be beginning to believe my explanation for not writing back. What I didn't know then was that his conversation with Matron had already made him a little suspicious and my reaction to what he had told me about my letters not arriving had more or less confirmed it. Still, as he understood how much his niece had gone through before she was placed in the home, he wanted to check me out a little more – just to be a hundred per cent certain that us meeting again would be good for her.

When I went back to the classroom, I was too excited at the thought of meeting Holly to even begin to concentrate on the subject being taught in that day's class. Instead, my head was filled with questions. What did she look like now? I was sure both of us had changed quite a lot. I might not have grown to the height I wanted to be, for I had stopped growing when I reached five feet. My hair was still the same shade of blonde, but my shape had changed – I wasn't flat-chested anymore! Something else that Emily Donaldson mocked me about. She kept giving me dirty looks and was fond of saying that I had begun to look like the girl I really was, a little blonde tart.

Just the thought of my foster mother popping into my head made me think of the phone call that Holly's Uncle John was going to make. I hated to think what she might tell him. She wouldn't have a nice word to say about me. I suddenly worried she might damn me so much that he would never return, let alone allow me to see Holly. But I need not have fretted for he had parked up and gave me such a wide smile when I bounced through the school gates – he even opened the car door for me.

'I haven't phoned your foster mother yet,' he told me as I was putting on my seat belt. 'I thought it was better if we met face to face so I'll drive you to where you live now and have a quick word with her. Then we can go out to a café I know and get something tasty to eat. I can tell you I'm desperate for some soda bread with thick Irish butter! Are you happy with that idea?'

My heart sank at the thought of Emily Donaldson meeting him. I knew how, with just a few words, she could make me look small, but there was nothing else I could say except OK.

I asked him a few questions about Holly as we drove there and he assured me she was doing well – 'She's made some nice friends' – and then after glancing quickly at me, he added, 'But she still talks about you nonstop.'

'I don't think you'll be invited in by Mrs Donaldson,' I said miserably, 'and she won't let me go out with you either.'

'Oh, she will, so just stop fretting. I've had a word with the matron for the home and she told me that you're a foster child, not an adopted one. Which means it's up to social services to give their permission for you to spend some time with Holly and me. Mrs Donaldson will know that so I'm pretty sure she will want to make a good impression on me.'

I liked the fact that he had said 'Holly and me' – it took away some of my nerviness.

'Funny, though, that she adopted your brother but not you,' John pondered, glancing over at me. 'By the way, where is he anyhow? I thought Michael would have been leaving school with you.'

'He's not at this one anymore,' I explained. 'They decided he would do better in a private school – they wanted the best education for him.'

'Best education for their *son*,' he said dryly. From the tone of his voice, I could tell he didn't approve of my brother being treated differently.

I began to feel with John being so friendly and understanding, after some consideration he now believed I had written those letters but that didn't stop me from trembling with nerves when we pulled up at the house.

'I'd best go in and tell her you're here,' I said hesitantly.

'Just open the door and call out to her, that would be better. I'll be standing right beside you, Gerri,' he told me.

I think for a moment Emily Donaldson thought he must be a teacher who had brought me back – she never went to my parents' evenings so she didn't know the teaching staff at all. With a warm smile, John greeted her and put out his hand for her to shake as he quickly introduced himself. He told her he wanted her permission on something, then asked if he could come in.

To my surprise she gave him one of her ladylike smiles and said yes.

'So, how can I help you?'

'I just want to take young Gerri out for something to eat so we can catch up. I want to be able to tell my niece that I've met her and that she's doing well.'

Another charming smile was proffered in her direction. I noticed that he didn't mention me meeting up with Holly. *Maybe he's doing it in stages*, I thought when I heard him saying how lovely the house was and what a lucky girl I was to be living there. He said yes to a cup of tea – a bit of a mistake as it gave my foster mother a reason to get me on my own.

'Come and give me a hand, will you, dear?'

She gave me just about the warmest smile she could manage. Once in the kitchen she hissed a warning to me: 'If you tell him a pack of lies, you'll get punished. I'll lock you in your room for the whole weekend and the following one too. That should make you think very carefully so be warned, Gerri.'

After she came in with the tray and poured the tea, he took a sip before saying to me, 'Now, Gerri, while I have this lovely tea, do you want to get changed out of your school uniform? I know we're going out to eat in a minute, but I can't resist this fruit cake.'

What could I say? There was nothing nice to wear in my room at all. Just a few second-hand, baggy and frayed things that I wore around the house when I was doing my chores. The only outfits I had that were fit to go out in were my Sunday grey suit or my school uniform, which I already had on.

I saw the expression of slight worry that flashed onto Emily Donaldson's face for just a second.

'Oh dear, I put some of her good outfits into the dry cleaner's this morning and the other stuff went in the washing machine just now,' she said quickly. 'She's a bit of a messy girl! What a nuisance you didn't come a couple of days later then they would all be ironed and hanging up.'

'Oh, not to worry' was his answer as she chatted a little about my school and then he stood up, said we would be off and he would bring me back in time to do my homework.

It was when we had finished eating our tea that he leant forward with his arms on the table and looked me in the eye.

'You'd better tell me what's been happening in that house over the last four years. Something isn't right and I don't believe a word she said about your clothes.'

Just the thought of explaining it all made me blink away tears, as did feeling a large warm hand gently touching mine.

'I can tell you're not happy there, Gerri.'

So, I told him about the letters and how Emily Donaldson always told me there was never one for me.

'And who posted all your letters to Holly?'

'She told me she had.'

He didn't say anything more about them then, that came later.

It was then that random bits of information about my

life with the Donaldsons burst out of me – how my foster mother knew about Ma's suicide and how she taunted me, saying her death was all my fault.

'Don't get upset, Gerri. I know about your childhood and how you had lost most of your memory. It's come back, hasn't it?'

'Yes,' I agreed.

'And did Mrs Donaldson help you get over that?'

Looking up at him, I saw through my tear-filled eyes that he knew she hadn't. I told him about Maureen then and how I so wished to see her.

'Because she knows more than you do?'

'Yes.'

After that, he stopped asking me any more questions about Mrs Donaldson and instead brought up my singing in the church choir.

'The head told me all about it,' he explained.

I said how kind the vicar and his wife were to me, then he talked a little about his own family, telling me how much they all enjoyed having Holly there and how his children saw her as a big sister. And finally came the words I so wanted to hear: he was going to take me to meet his niece.

'I'll have another quick word with Mrs Donaldson when we get back then we can arrange to take you out for the weekend. I'll even tell her not to worry about getting your clothes ready, as I suspect there are none but I will simply say that Holly has brought you some of her favourites that she's outgrown. This is not the time to put her in an embarrassing situation.'

Not that I guessed then, but he was already making plans to help me.

'And I will see Holly again?'

'Absolutely you will.'

60

It was when we were back at the house that John brought up the subject of me spending the weekend with him and his niece. He made sure my foster mother understood it could only happen that weekend as he had to go back to England for work after that and his niece had only been allowed to have a week out of school. She looked a little doubtful as she considered his request and for a few seconds, she didn't say a word.

But John realised she was doing as expected: searching for the right excuse to say no – 'Oh, I understand you don't know me from Adam. Luckily, social services do – very well, in fact. I spent some time with them being vetted as a suitable guardian when I was arranging to take my niece back to the UK. As I understand Gerri is a foster child, not an adopted one, it's up to social services to give permission. I can make a phone call when I get back to my friends. I have Julia Macbride's private phone number in my diary – she's the one who helped my niece and me.

I'm sure you might have met her – I know she visits some of the homes where there are foster children. I think that getting her permission would make you happier, wouldn't it? So Mrs Donaldson, what I propose is that after I've spoken to Julia, I'll ask her to get in touch with you. Now …' and he stood up swiftly, 'I think I'd better get moving – Holly will be desperate for news of Gerri.'

'Please don't go just yet,' Emily Donaldson said brightly, 'let's make our own arrangements. There's no need for you to bother Julia.'

Triumphant, I tried my best not to let a knowing smirk settle on my face. That was the first time I had seen Emily squirm.

'It's not that I don't know who you are, John – I've heard a lot about Holly and how Gerri here misses her.'

Yes, of course she read your letters. This is your chance to have some fun, Gerri. Be careful not to upset her now, Ma was telling me.

'It was good of you to sort out my clothes,' I told my foster mother with the first smile I had given her since I was moved into the garage, 'but John told me that as Holly is a little older, she's brought loads of her things for me and I'm sure they'll fit. All I'm going to need is some underwear and a toothbrush.'

Good girl!

'Gerri, if it's all good with you both, I'll pick you up from school on Friday afternoon,' John told me.

Not so much as a peep came out of Emily Donaldson's lips. She must have known that she could be facing trouble with social services, so the best thing was to let him do as he wanted. But he hadn't finished yet.

'Ah, by the way, where's young Michael? I met him in the home – nice boy and Holly liked him as well.'

A question that was bound to make her uneasy, as he intended. The last thing she would want was him meeting up with Michael. My brother might just drop a few remarks that could be embarrassing.

'He's staying over with one of his friends tonight so they can do their homework together,' she explained.

'Sounds good.'

With that thought to ponder, John shook her hand to confirm the arrangements, said his goodbyes and left the house.

* * *

Naturally, before the weekend came, there were many more threats from my agitated foster mother but for once I wasn't afraid. From the tight expression on her face, she knew that. Thursday came and went and then it was Friday, the day John was going to take me to see Holly. To my surprise, Emily told me she would make sure I got up early so I could have a shower and do my hair and that I might as well have breakfast in the kitchen with the family. In fact, as her husband was driving my brother to school, she would drive me to mine as it would be quicker than catching the bus. Was I hearing right? I guessed she wanted me to look as neat and tidy as possible for my visit.

In other words, I would appear well looked after.

When the school day eventually came to a close I must have been first out of the classroom – I was in such a hurry to go. I rushed to the gates and just about leapt into John's car.

The journey took about an hour until we drove into Portrush, the seaside town that I had wanted to visit for so long.

'You and Holly can go for a walk along that promenade tomorrow,' he told me as he drove past it. I could see mile upon mile of pale sand and white foam on the waves as they broke near the shoreline. It brought back some of my happy childhood memories and I gulped with happiness.

'We're staying at this hotel for the weekend,' he told me as he turned the car into a long drive. In front of me I saw a large grey stone house, with huge wooden doors held open by a carved wooden doorstop. 'I booked Holly a room with two beds in it, so you two will have plenty of time to catch up. Expect you'll still be chatting when dawn comes,' he said with another one of his friendly grins.

What a meeting it was when we walked through the door to find an excited Holly waiting for us in the foyer. She looked both radiant and tearful the moment her eyes met mine.

'I can't believe you're here at last, Gerri,' she said, while I could hardly get a word out, as tears of joy streamed down my face.

'And I couldn't be happier being here,' I sobbed as for a moment we held each other at arm's length to take a good look at how much we had changed. Of course, we no longer looked the same. We had both grown a few inches and our bodies were a completely different shape, but apart from that we would have recognised each other wherever we had met.

Holly's dark hair was now in a thick shiny bob and those blue eyes of hers that must have run in the family sparkled away. There was no doubt that she was really lovely and I could see that she was happy as well.

When she took me up to our room the first thing I spotted was a pretty deep-blue dress lying on my bed.

'I remembered blue was your favourite colour,' she told me, which made me hug her again.

'It's so pretty, thank you,' I said, feeling more tears coming.

I hadn't had anything I liked, far less brand new, since I left the home. It turned out not only had she brought her old clothes for me, but her uncle had also bought the dress that Holly had chosen. She explained that he had described what they must have guessed to be my height and build to the lady at the shop and she agreed to change it if it didn't fit. Not only that, he had told Holly to take me shopping the next day for some more clothes after handing her a large wad of cash.

It was the second time in less than half an hour that I was close to tears. After all, thoughtfulness and kindness like that were hardly what I was used to. I can remember putting the dress on and then staring in the mirror at what I thought was a different me. Holly lent me a pair of shoes that might have been a bit tight, but I didn't care – school sandals hardly did the dress justice. I felt much more confident when I walked down the broad wooden staircase into the dining room, where the three of us were having an early supper. As I sat down, I thanked John effusively.

'It's my pleasure. Holly chose it,' he said. 'And I have to say she has good taste; you look really pretty in it.'

'Thanks,' I muttered as I felt my cheeks turn a bright red. I don't think anyone had paid me a compliment in the last four years.

The evening was fun. We didn't talk about Emily Donaldson, nor did John mention that while Holly and I were going sightseeing and shopping, he had an appointment with the vicar to see what he could learn from him and his wife about my situation.

* * *

Holly and I had a total blast walking through that town. She insisted on lending me a pair of frayed pale-blue jeans and a yellow top – 'Can't walk around in your school uniform or a party dress, can you? Breakfast first and then out we go. A walk will do us good before we hit the shops,' she told me excitedly.

She had already earmarked the shop where I could find the right clothes. Her generous uncle had given her enough to buy me a whole new wardrobe. Jeans, a couple of sweaters and a denim jacket were sent into the changing room, followed by some blouses and a blue denim midi skirt.

After marching out with all those shopping bags between us, Holly now took me into a shoe shop – 'Flatties are in and they look good with jeans and dresses.' She certainly knew more about fashion than me.

'Goodness knows what Mrs Donaldson is going to say to all this,' I told her.

'Who cares? They're your clothes,' she told me blithely. 'Now, let's go for coffee and a cake, shall we? All that shopping and sea air has made me starving!'

Coffee ordering was down to Holly and it came in a tall glass cup with a covering of creamy foam, something I had never tasted before. 'Yummy!' I told her and she laughed as my top lip was covered in white foam.

'Where's your bedroom in the house?' she suddenly asked, making me nearly choke. 'Come on, Gerri. Are you sleeping upstairs in that house or not?'

Her question surprised me so much, my mouth fell open.

'You're not then, are you?'

'No,' I said.

'Just tell me,' she coaxed.

So I did – I couldn't help myself. Over another coffee and a slab of cake, she managed to wheedle just about everything out of me.

'But she mustn't ever know I've told you anything. That would get me in so much trouble,' I told her anxiously.

Holly didn't ask what the trouble might be. Instead her hand moved over the table to hold mine.

'Don't worry, Gerri. Trust me, nothing bad's going to happen. Now let's just enjoy our day out.'

'How did you guess?' I wanted to know.

'Oh, my uncle has sharp eyes. He glanced through the garage window as he left and saw a part of it had been sectioned off and how she spoke for you when he suggested you get changed. Any other girl would have run upstairs to get out of her uniform – having me about has taught him a little about how teenagers think.'

I was simply loving being with Holly and her uncle. The only thing spoiling the day was the thought that I would be going back to the Donaldsons' the following lunchtime – Holly and her uncle were going in the afternoon so that she would be back at school on the Monday.

It was Sunday morning when we were finishing breakfast that John told me he needed to talk to me. Hearing this, Holly gave me a reassuring pat on my arm and said she would be in our room when we were finished.

'I went to see the vicar yesterday,' he began, 'and he told me a few things, like how they got social services round when some bruises were noticed on you. They thought you were a troubled little girl when they first met you, which is why they did the best they could to help. Gerri, if you're in agreement, I've made up my mind not to take you back to the Donaldsons' – unless that's not what you want to do.'

'I don't ever want to go back,' I told him.

'Good,' he said. 'I'm going to talk to both the Donaldsons about what I've learnt. Oh, no doubt about it, she'll call you a liar but I will stand my ground. She's adopted your brother and she won't want social services coming in and causing problems over that, not when they will want to see your bedroom. I don't think your brother would lie about that either.'

'He doesn't know how she treats me.'

'She still won't want the trouble it could give her.'

I could hardly believe what I was hearing.

'So, where will I go?' I asked, my heart already pounding in the hope that I would be going with them.

'I want you to finish your exams at the school you're at,' he told me. 'At the moment, Ireland has a slightly different education system so it's best if you finish here but at Christmas and for the long summer holidays, you will come to us. And when your exams are over, if you still want to, I will bring you over to England. Now, how does that sound?'

Speechless, I could hardly stop my tears from flowing. A tissue was gently pushed into my hand.

'I'll drop you at the vicar's house while I talk to the Donaldsons as soon as they're back from church,' he continued. 'The vicar has arranged accommodation for you and social services are with us all the way. It only took one phone call. A vicar friend of his, who has two children and luckily a spare room, will let you stay there.'

The last question he asked was whether there was anything in my room that I might want.

'The doll,' I said firmly, 'it was my mother's. My books and my satchel.'

And two years later, after I had taken my exams, he and Holly came over to collect me. The vicar's house had been a friendly place where I spent a happy few months.

His own children were away at university so I hardly ever saw them but he and his wife had welcomed me in and seemed to like having me at their home – I certainly found it easier to concentrate on my homework there. Although I was eager to move on, I was sad to say goodbye to them.

There was just one thing I had to do before I left Ireland.

Visit Maureen.

61

Those two years in Ireland went by faster than I thought possible. I had passed what was called Junior Certificate Exams, which was almost the same as GCEs, except that we had to pass more than one subject to be awarded it. The next step would be to take my education further in England. I needed to be accepted on a course for the profession I wished to be part of – I was going to be a nurse, as my mother had been.

Even though that time spent at the vicar's house had been pleasant enough, I could hardly wait to leave. I would keep in touch with Michael, and he and I had even managed to meet several times. A year younger, he was still at school. He never asked why I had moved out, any more than I told him what I thought of Emily Donaldson. He knew about me meeting Holly and my visits to her; he just said once that if I moved there, I must keep in touch.

I just loved being with Holly and her family when I was with them for holidays. John's wife Marion made me so welcome that I already felt part of the family. Each time I left Ireland all the trauma of my past seemed much further away. The one thing that bothered me was that there were still unanswered questions and I wanted to fill in those gaps before I finally left Ireland for what I was determined to be the last time. The only person who could give the answers to what had happened that night was Maureen and I needed to understand why Ma had done what she had done and the other facts as to the aftermath of that tumultuous event as well. I had the questions planted in my mind, I was just waiting for answers. Where had my father gone? What had happened to the priest? I was haunted by the thought of Father Pat being relocated in another parish and getting to know other small children. And the other really important question was whether Maureen had any news of my two young brothers and if she had addresses – I so wanted to meet them again.

* * *

Six years after Emily Donaldson first accused me of being responsible for my mother's death, I finally discovered the truth about her suicide. It was John who arranged the meeting with Maureen. Not at her house, where so many memories lay, but in the hotel where he was staying. He said he thought that would be better for both of us. I hadn't told Michael that we would be meeting up – I was reluctant to do so.

So, I waited in the hotel foyer for John to return from the station as he had gone to fetch her. The minute

Maureen walked in, I felt such a lump in my throat. I couldn't help myself, I simply flew into her arms and hugged her. The words 'I've missed you so much' tumbled from both our lips.

She looked almost tearful as she said, 'I thought I had done the best for you by staying away, which doesn't mean I never wanted to see you.'

We went into the visitors' lounge then, which was quiet and peaceful, while John arranged tea for both of us. Once it came, he left us alone so we could chat in private.

Maureen told me then that part of her had wanted to have me living with her: 'But that was not my sensible part, Gerri,' she conceded. 'I knew it would be better for you if you lived in a completely different area.'

I had a shrewd idea why that was after my experience with Emily Donaldson.

'You mean parents wouldn't have wanted me mixing with their children because I might have told them dirty things?'

'Not all people would have been like that, but there's no point in denying that some of them would have been. Also, I had to consider if you would have been happy staying in the village. Not only would you have heard some gossip about your mother, but every day you would have seen the house where you and your family had lived. I thought that would have stopped you putting anything behind you.'

I then brought up the subject of my brothers and she told me that Keith, the youngest one, had been adopted but she didn't know the adoptive couple's names and that my middle brother, Pete, was with foster parents. She promised that she would write to them; she believed once Pete was a little older, his foster parents would let him get in touch with me – 'And your youngest brother, Keith, might try and search for his family as well, when he turns eighteen.'

As for my father, he was somewhere in England and no, she didn't have his address.

'I wouldn't want it anyhow,' I said with conviction.

'Good, you're doing the right thing there, Gerri.'

'And the priest?' I asked.

'He fled, we know that – but where he went, I have no idea. I made sure the Catholic Church knew about him so they would get rid of him. If not, they would have to keep an eye on him.'

I felt numb at that, but at least I would never see him again. Maureen added that she had done some research and he was no longer with the Church. Once I knew the answers to those questions, I brought up the biggest question that had saddened me for so long. And if you have come to this part of my story, I'm sure you will also be wondering why my mother chose to leave us the way she did, instead of just going to the police and asking for help. Here, I have to delve a little into Irish history for you to fully understand the context, so if it's familiar to you, please indulge me.

Today, many people see Ireland as a beautiful, peaceful place with amazing scenery but that's not how it was talked about in the 1960s and 70s. Not when the IRA were setting off bombs in England and the death toll was rising. But unless you were around at that time, I expect you see it as distant history. I can say though that it caused a huge problem in my life. You see, Northern Ireland was in the midst of a thirty-year conflict that has become known as the Troubles. I would say it was more of a civil war in Ulster, one waged between the armed military wings of both the Catholics and the Protestants. The British Army were sent over to try and keep the peace, as well as trying to protect the warring communities. I was probably six or seven when I realised that the Catholics were fighting for what they thought of as their freedom while the other side, the Protestants, were doing their very best to stop them.

Just about every day there were riots and I remember my parents listening anxiously to the news. There were people, such as the ones in our village, who believed that if we all just stayed in the Catholic areas, the rioters and the police would have little interest in us. Luckily, as we were not part of a large town, our small village remained peaceful.

The civil rights movement, with heavy support from Irish-Catholic Americans, demanded an end to discrimination against Catholics in voting rights, housing and employment. It was the lack of those rights which had caused not just riots, but many brutal deaths as well. Eventually they were granted these rights. Up to then there had been many places where Catholics could neither rent nor buy a house. As for jobs, it was deemed acceptable then for newspaper advertisements to clearly state that only Protestants need apply – and that was the polite version. So, it's hardly surprising really that the conflict became much larger and more violent with both sides to blame for the number of deaths that took place.

One of the greatest fears the Catholics had was of the police. They saw them as a gang of hardened Protestants who were totally against them and took a great delight in arresting them for the slightest reason. Which may or may not have been true, but that is how they felt. So, I think you can understand why anger towards the Royal Ulster Constabulary, as the police were called, was brewing in the Catholic areas.

In those days a Catholic woman like my mother would have been far too scared to have walked into a police station and I still have no idea how they would have reacted to her, especially given the crime she would be reporting. Even worse for Ma was that she had been brought up in a Protestant family, who had disowned her when she married my Catholic father. I believe that she may have risked it, had it not been for Bloody Sunday having just taken place on 30 January 1972. Masses of stones were thrown at the group of soldiers by a large ring of men, many of the culprits little more than children. Maybe those soldiers believed they would be killed if they didn't fight back. All we know is that the army retaliated with tear gas, water cannons and rubber bullets. To begin with. And then panic set in and real bullets were shot from their guns. Fourteen people died, all of them Catholics, and many more were injured that day. The Catholics were up in arms and after that, the police and the army had their hands full.

'That happened the year you were rushed into hospital.

It was all the riots after that and the number of men from both sides being thrown into prison that put a huge pressure on the police,' Maureen told me. 'It was that which must have made your mother believe that the police would not help, they would just see a hysterical Catholic woman trying to cause even more trouble. And yes, I can understand that.

'Gerri, I swear to you that she never told me what she had planned. Of course, I rushed over when I heard the sirens coming to fetch you. She just asked if I could look after the boys for a few days and said that you were going to the hospital. So, after she refused my offer to stay with her a while, I went back to my house.

'What she did later that evening was to put several letters through my door. One was for your father and two others were for the police and social services. Then there was one for me explaining what she wanted me to do: I was to use those letters to make your father do as she wished. The letter to him was very clear: he had to sign those adoption forms. If not, the other letters would put him in prison. She really believed it was the best she could do for you and the boys. Had I known the full extent of what was in her head, I would have stopped her, Gerri, I promise I would, but I didn't know.'

'How did she do it?'

'Sleeping pills. After she took them, she went upstairs and slept in your room. Your da would not have gone in there, not after all that had happened. When eventually he did, she was gone.'

Both of us had tears streaming down our cheeks.

Maureen handed me a wad of tissues and eventually our sobs ceased as we took a moment to reflect on the enormity of that conversation.

So, did I think my mother did the right thing? No, but at least now and over the years to come I was able to understand a little more about why she died as she did. After all, hadn't her voice in my dreams prepared me a little? Maybe it had but I never really understood until I learned about the letters she had left behind. So often in my life I had wanted to escape a world I had every reason to hate and be reunited with her. It was not until I met up with Maureen again that I really understood Ma's reasons for leaving this earth as she did.

She was determined that none of her children would live with their father. Up until then, I had never really understood why we were all taken from the place where we were born, where we had each other and friends in our community for support. But now I did. My mother's wish for us was that we would all be adopted by people who would treat us as their own. Not only had she put that in writing, but she forced our father, a man she was once deeply in love with but no longer trusted, to give up his rights to us as well. She even made him put that in writing. Until Maureen talked to me, I had never realised that it was Ma who had wanted us to be removed from the family home. To this day, I still find it hard to accept how she went about her plans.

Once she had cleaned me up and settled me, she called for an ambulance. As she waited for it to come, she wrote the letters and delivered them to Maureen with instructions of what to do with them. She told her friend the bare minimum: only that she wanted her children to be taken away from their father because of his drinking and asked her to keep the boys for the night, saying she still had things to organise. In reality, this was so her suicide wouldn't be discovered.

I can't help but wonder why she chose such a dreadful way to end her life. Didn't she realise we all loved her? My baby brother must have cried and cried when he knew that he would never see her again.

Didn't she stop and wonder who would bring us all up? Without her, who would teach my brothers to be decent young men? And what about me, her only daughter? Wasn't I the child who needed her most? She must have known that suicide in a small Catholic town would cause an outrageous scandal – big enough to ensure we could no longer stay there.

Maureen told me that she had no idea what Ma was planning and the letters remained sealed. She assured me that my mother had her reasons for not wanting to involve the police but if push came to shove and her plan didn't work, letters would be posted informing the authorities of her husband's deeds. Which is why she entrusted them with her dearest and closest friend, a woman who loved her children almost as much as she did.

How she arranged every detail has never come to light for what remains missing from the puzzle is the letter she wrote to Da. What I do know is that she knew exactly what had taken place between me, my father and Father Pat as she committed the words to paper.

Just how did she feel when she walked into that room after the priest fled? For there was her intoxicated, half-naked daughter, dress over her head, legs and body exposed and streaked in blood and vomit. Her only daughter, almost unconscious with shock and trauma. Meanwhile, her husband was slumped in a chair, so drunk not a word he said made sense. I doubt she chose to listen to his feeble excuses – what he had been party to was all too evident.

Once the letters had been dealt with, she sat in her favourite chair and swallowed the pills that, as a nurse, she had in her possession.

So, was it Da who phoned for the ambulance on that fateful night, or was it Maureen?

I still don't know. What I do know now is that my mother was dead before the ambulance carrying her reached the same hospital where I was undergoing surgery.

Maybe she too was in shock and unable to think straight so she had no idea that death was close to hand. That's what I like to believe anyway. What consoles me a little is the knowledge that the two men who knew everything are no longer in this world.

Their wicked secrets left with them.

Not that the man I can scarcely bring myself to call my father left this earth peacefully.

*   *   *

Maureen had arranged to stay the night in the same hotel as John and I so we were able to spend more time together.

'When are you going?' she asked.

'Tomorrow,' I told her.

We said we would keep in touch and hugged each other tightly when she left. John came to say goodbye to her too.

'Has that helped?' he asked.

'It's cleared my head a little,' was all I could say although I was grateful to him for his support.

An hour later, we were at the airport. As we boarded the plane, I felt as if I was walking into a new life.

I'm coming too, darlin'. I told you I would always be with you.

I felt a warm glow and smiled as we took our seats. As the plane took off, I looked down at the lights of Belfast.

Goodbye, I whispered silently.

Epilogue

So, how were all those years that lay ahead of me after I stepped onto the plane? I suppose you might say it was a mixture of ups and downs. I understand now that up until my thirties, it was my past that caused me to crave love. There were too many times when after only a few weeks I realised the passion I felt for the latest boyfriend was completely one-sided and each time that was made clear to me, I was heartbroken. Situations that happened all too often. It was when I accepted the affair was over that I turned to drink – I remembered how the alcohol I had been given as a child had soothed away my pain and the adult me decided to turn to it again.

I was lucky to have Holly as a friend. Each time it happened, she was patient and helped me out of my dark spell. When the days seemed bright again, I felt I owed her so much. If she hadn't persuaded her uncle to find me, where would I have ended up? That's a question I dare not think too much about. And thanks to Holly and her uncle, I also had a career I loved – nursing.

I took the courses that were needed to become a nurse:

NVQ 1, 2 and 3. At eighteen I was being trained by senior nurses in the local hospital. Over the years I worked in nursing care and on psychiatry. In my twenties a large part of my work was caring for terminally ill patients, making their last days as peaceful as possible. I gave support to their loved ones, who sat by their side until the very end.

I also sat by the beds of those who had taken overdoses and I knew this was often a cry for help. A cry for help that I understood. When their eyes flicked open, I would hold their hand and try and comfort them a little. The one ward I asked not to be on was the children's ward – I just couldn't bear the thought of seeing little ones seriously ill.

Right from the start I made good friends in the hospitals I worked in and meanwhile, Holly was always there for me. She was now learning to become a teacher. But over the years I never stopped hoping that one day I would meet my brothers again.

Michael kept in touch during those early years. He contacted me when our father was rushed into hospital in the early nineties – I had no idea when their contact had started up again but he was travelling over to see him and wanted me to come as well.

'He's dying,' he told me.

And he nearly had me killed, I felt like saying. Instead I just said I had no wish to see him and that was the beginning of Michael and me finally drifting apart. But I did see my brother one more time. By then he was the spitting image of Da and it didn't take me long to see that he had more than just his father's looks for he too had become a heavy drinker. He had blocked the years when we were close from his mind.

That was the last I heard of him.

As my youngest brother had been adopted, I was able to trace him once I came of age. I wrote to him but he replied saying he had a family and wasn't interested in meeting anyone from the family he had been born into. At that point I gave up and accepted the fact that it was unlikely I would ever see my brothers again. Imagine how I felt when in my early thirties a letter dropped through the letter box. I could hardly believe that after so many years my middle brother Pete had finally found me! I can't tell you how happy I was when I read his letter saying how he wanted to come and see me. Of course I rang the phone number on the letter at once and arranged for him to come and visit me.

I was just about shaking with nerves as I waited at the station. *Would we recognise each other?* When the train pulled in and the passengers walked through the barrier, I saw a tall man with thick blond hair in a ponytail coming towards me.

'You're Gerri, aren't you?' he said with such a wide happy smile that I found myself giving him an enormous hug.

For five years we were close. He never married and just did whatever odd jobs he could for work. A heavy drinker, I suspect he took drugs as well but I never stopped loving him.

One of the saddest things that happened in my adult life was when I received a phone call to tell me that Pete had died of heart failure. He was only in his early thirties, which convinced me that drugs must have been a part of it. I was truly devastated. His death made me concentrate more on my work and I really put my heart into it, having given up the idea that I was ever going to have a happy relationship.

And then a miracle happened.

I met the right man, one who has made me happy for so long.

I'll let him tell you how we met...

My Meeting Gerri

Gerri and I met at a mutual friend's house on 16 June 2009. Being a typical man, I didn't read the signs and was totally unaware that we had been set up. Gerri had to literally spell it out to me that she was trying to chat me up! I ended up giving her a lift home and arranging to meet the following Saturday to sort out her laptop. While looking at her laptop, she said that I could read her book that she had been writing for a few years – it was her way of coming to terms with what happened to her over the years.

By the end of it I was in tears and it was at that point we had our first kiss. A short time after this we had our first proper date at the Maybush in Waldringfield. We had a lovely meal and afterwards decided to have a stroll down by the river. Unfortunately, there are some concrete steps down to the riverbank, which Gerri fell down and grazed her knee. So, we walked along the riverbank until we came to a bench and as we sat there, she decided to remove her stocking, which also got damaged in the fall.

Being the gentleman, I looked the other way. Once she had removed the first stocking, she decided the other one would have to come off as well so again I looked the other way. On the way back to the Maybush we could see everyone watching to see if there was going to be any repeat of before but they were disappointed as we made an almost-perfect ascent of the steps – we didn't go back there for some time after that!

I used to visit Gerri frequently at her flat in Ipswich and we had some great times together. One day around Christmas 2009 she wasn't feeling very well so I invited her to stay with me for a few days while she got better. We got on so well that I asked her to move in permanently, which she did and to save money, she gave up her flat.

In June 2010 we went to India with some friends for two weeks, which was amazing. Things were ticking along nicely but I sensed there was still a bit of insecurity with Gerri so on 1 September 2012, I popped the question, to which she replied yes. Over the past three years we had become very close and I had fallen in love with her. Exactly one year later to the day, 1 September 2013, we married over the anvil at Gretna Green in front of our families and friends – around thirty people, which was a huge surprise to me. When we first started to plan the wedding, it was going to be a small gathering but Gerri had other ideas and behind my back planned the whole thing, which was a day I will never forget. Everything was perfect that day and the following day, we set off on honeymoon to Majorca for ten days.

Married life was wonderful and we couldn't love each other more. Then in January 2017, Gerri had a fall at the top of the stairs and broke her back – a big blow to both of us and this was to have a great impact on our relationship. Following surgery to repair her back, which involved rods and screws to hold her lower spine together, she spent six months on a hospital bed in our living room with me as her main carer. Thankfully she wasn't paralysed from the waist down and in time was able to start walking again.

Most relationships would probably have suffered in this situation but ours grew even stronger. Gerri relied on me to do almost everything for her at the start of her recovery but now she has become much more independent again. We still have a way to go but I'm sure that in time she will be back to her old self. We still enjoy lots of things together and have had some fantastic holidays. We've been to Mexico, Majorca and Greece since the accident and have also been for days away in the UK. As we both near retirement, there are plans for many more adventures. Gerri had a right knee replacement in May 2021 and is now on the list for the left knee. Once this is complete, there will be no stopping us. It won't be long before we are walking down the street hand in hand again with no support but each other. I doubt if I could love her more.

Acknowledgements

Gerri: There are so many people I could thank for this book, and I am sorry if I have missed any of you. I couldn't have got here without the incredible support from family and friends and I am so grateful for each and every one of you.

This book has been a real journey and I couldn't have done it without Toni Maguire, who has believed in me from the start and, in doing so, has allowed this story to be told.

Lastly, I want to thank my family. My darling husband, Paul, who has turned my life around and my wonderful stepchildren who have accepted me into their lives, you have made my world a better place.

Toni: Thanks to my friend, Caroline Bagley, who has given me hours of her time, in reading through these stories and giving me advice.

Finally, from both of us: Thanks so much to everyone involved in the publishing process: our editor, Ciara Lloyd; copy editor, Jane Donovan; and agent, Barbara Levy. Your help and support has been invaluable every step of the way.